Cold Feat

How I froze my mid-life crisis right off...

Jason Donnelly

Hillerød, Denmark

I started putting this book together in my head in a thousand-liter water tank on February 14th, 2023. The water surrounding my body was roughly 4 degrees Celsius and when I say "roughly," I mean it. It's rough putting your body into water that cold.

Dedicated to anyone who's just getting warmed up…

Table of Contents

Chapter 6: The Upward Turn: Catching the Lifeline of Cold Baths

Introducing the game-changing practice of cold bathing as a means of overcoming a mid-life crisis. It outlines the benefits of this practice (specifically with mental fortitude) and tips on how to start safely.

Chapter 7: Reconstruction: "The Weight Loss Chapter"

Covering the holistic plan for rejuvenation through a healthier lifestyle, including diet, exercise, and weight loss tips. It offers guidance on staying committed to this journey. *hint, it's cold bathing

Chapter 8: Working Through: From Turbulence to Tranquility

Helping readers understand how to work through their mid-life crisis with actionable strategies for motivation and resilience, encouraging them to view the crisis as a transition rather than an end.

Chapter 9: Acceptance: Embracing the Mid-Life Enlightenment

Highlighting the importance of acceptance in managing a mid-life crisis and offering practical steps on how to transform this acceptance into a source of strength and peace.

Chapter 10: Hope: The Bright Light at the End of the Mid-Life Tunnel

Talking about the role of hope in overcoming a mid-life crisis. It uses real-life stories and practical exercises to help the reader create a sense of optimism for the future.

Chapter 11: The Ice Bathing Club: Finding Your Tribe

Discover how to build and benefit from a supportive community when dealing with life's transitions. Filled with uplifting stories direct from the ice bathing community.

Chapter 12: Lawyer-Forced Safety Chapter
The required chapter covering safety measures and precautions to be followed during cold bathing. Because the last thing we want is for you to get hurt.

PREFACE

August 20, 2023

It took 200 days to get to this date, which makes no sense if you just picked this book up off the shelf all willy-nilly.

You know what? This isn't a solid start. Let me start over.

If you're following me on my Cold Feat social channels (or have been stalking me) you know that August 20th, 2023 is the 200th day in a row of throwing my previously chunky body into cold water. Not like, a chilly pool of cold water, but water so cold that it makes your vascular system push as much of your blood as it can to your core because it wants to make sure you don't die.

Read that again.

I'll wait.

For 200 days, I've purposely gotten into water so cold that my body thinks it needs to protect me. What kind of psychopath does that kind of thing?

If we're to believe the internet and various news channels, a lot of people.

That being said, I am not a navy seal, I haven't broken any world records, and for all intents and purposes, you could consider me a pretty normal guy. For my day job, I work in marketing as a writer, I have a two-and-a-half-year-old son named Jameson, and my partner's name is Anna.

No one forced me to take this thing on. And even now, I don't think it's something I'm "taking on" rather, I'm doing it because it's changed my life. And the contributors on the cover? It changed their lives too.

Cold bathing is so much more than just getting in some cold water, it does something to your wiring. And when I say that, I don't mean physically (although it might), I mean mentally. Things change.

That's why the book is set up the way it is. Each chapter is built around Elisabeth Kübler-Ross' 7 stages of grief, with a little massaging to drag it out to 10. Shock, Denial, Pain, Bargaining, Depression, The Upward Turn, Reconstruction, Working Through, Acceptance, and Hope.

I don't think that anyone decides to do what I've done without something breaking inside. We'll get to my reasons soon but understand that the only way you're going to get to the other side of whatever broke is by going through it.

It sucks. But it's worth it. Trust me, I'm on the other side.

Lastly, before we dive into the real book, I have to clear up what Cold Feat is and what it's not…

Most importantly, it isn't a spelling mistake! I didn't just want to focus on feet, but the feat of getting in cold water, even though there are feet everywhere… you get it.

Definition
noun
Combination of "cold feet" and "feat."
- Cold feet: a doubt strong enough to prevent a planned course of action.
- Feat: an achievement that requires great courage, skill, or strength.

Getting into water this cold? Well, that's a cold feat, and a lot of us are doing it every day to help us physically, mentally, or all of the above.

In the following pages, we'll see what a mid-life crisis looked like through my eyes, what losing my mother-in-law meant, how cold bathing jumpstarted a new chapter of my life, which container(s) I settled on, why I started breathwork, and a step-by-step guide to how I lost over 60 pounds and changed my entire life trajectory in only a few short months.

There's also chapter 11, an entire chapter dedicated to some of my favorite ice bathers from around the world. Every day, they inspire me, and I hope their stories do the same for you. Please seek them out across social and see why I love them so much. This community is incredible.

Finally, just so you're prepared for it, each chapter is broken into around 5 sections:

- An intro from yours truly (the memoir part)

- 2-4 sections on understanding what's going on, the science, how to handle it, and ideas I've found that help

- A summary of the chapter if you just can't find the time to read the whole sha-bang

I figure that some of you beautiful people will want to read the memoir only, some don't care about me and want to hear about the crisis, others only want to know about ice bathing or weight loss, and others yet, just want to read the stories from my ice bathing friends.

Read it however makes you happy. This is your book now. Heck, some of you might not even read this part…

Chapter 1: Shock

"The Uninvited Guest"

I. Introduction (The memoir part)

I am not special.

I know… that's probably not the sentence you're looking for in the first chapter of a motivational book about freezing off your mid-life crisis, but hear me out. From the day I was born, I've been told that I am special, I think a lot of us have. And for some reason, despite the very clear facts that say otherwise, I believed it.

In a book dedicated to breathing and ice baths, I have to mention Wim Hof at least once, but this will be my only mention. Like him, I was born out of necessity. I was removed from my mother due to the umbilical cord being wrapped around my neck. When I came out, I had black and blue marks around my little body. Interestingly, it was only a few hours before President Reagan was shot. A lot of people forget that he was shot on March 30th, 1981, at 2:27 pm. If my parents forgot, it's okay, they were busy with something else at the time, but you dear reader, should know better.

Like a lot of people born around this time, I have a very distinct mix of generational characteristics. Part Gen X and part Millennial, sometimes being called Xennials because everything these days needs a name, but honestly, my generational subset doesn't associate with either fully.

We grew up without the internet, but in our teenage years were introduced to dial-up modems and AOL instant messenger. A/S/L? Computers were a thing and we had typing classes, but up until that point, we played outside and many of us fought cell phones because why would we need them? Our entire life we told our parents where we were going, came back (usually) when we said we would, and called them from payphones if necessary. I remember in my twenties defiantly telling people that I didn't have a cell phone and if they called me at home and I wasn't there, I was busy, I'd get back to them when I wasn't.

We were the generation that moved from eight-tracks to cassette tapes and religiously recorded our favorite songs from the radio, hoping to not have the DJ talking over the beginning or the end of songs.

The generation that embraced social media, but remembers life before it. We bridged the technological gap and to tell you the truth, don't like to be called millennials because we're not.

Jason, what does this have to do with a mid-life crisis, you ask? Well, at the time of this writing, I'm 42 years old, overweight, and balding. A little over a year ago I moved from Brooklyn, New York to a city on the outskirts of Copenhagen, Denmark with my fiance and son, and in 30 days (which I didn't know when typing this) one of my favorite people on the planet will die of cancer.

Can I just say fuck cancer, or should I wait until we get further into the book? Both? Perfect. Fuck cancer.

If the thoughts and feelings I'm having every day aren't a mid-life crisis, the proverbial fat lady is warming up. *It should also probably be said that if referencing a hypothetical fat lady warming up offends you, pick another book, it's not going to get lighter. Then again, there aren't a lot of books on ice baths and mid-life crises, so you may just have to deal with it. I apologize in advance (but most likely don't mean it).

Anywho, as the chapter is named, my mid-life crisis was a bit of a shock, and it all stemmed from a simple comment from a twenty-something man at the DMV (or whatever it's called in Denmark). I had to forfeit my New York driver's license to the Danish government to get a Danish license. For said license, I got my picture taken. The young man behind the counter told me where to stand, told me I couldn't smile, and the other fun details of getting your picture taken on a government document, and when the flash went off and the photo shot up onto a digital frame, he asked, "is the pic okay?"

I looked over at the screen and thought to myself, "Wow, I look like fresh dog shit" (my inner monologue is rough, I'm working on it), and asked him if we could take another.

He did, I looked at the picture, and surprisingly, still looked exactly like the first picture. Being the nice young man that he was, he asked, "How about that one?"

Outloud, I said very matter of factly that, "Yeah, I guess that's just what I look like now."

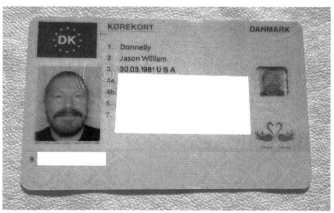

I look like an overweight alcoholic with a hygiene problem. It makes me sad to see that guy.

I don't think he understood the depth of what I was saying or why I was saying it at all, but that was the first moment in my life that I truly realized (or let myself understand) that I was getting older. And that I wasn't really taking care of myself.

"There are plenty of other indicators that I'm getting older. Thank you for bringing this up…" I say to myself, as the only person writing this book.

To be very clear to all you youngin's reading this, getting older hurts, no one tells you this. Oh, they tell you that they're sore, or how their joints ache here and there, but no one really tells you how much it hurts. I'm guessing that this comes from the fact that no one cares. Think about it. I tell you x, y, and z hurts, and what will you do? Apologize that my body hurts. Ask if there's something you can do.

You can't.

But the more mornings that I woke up in real pain, the more I decided I couldn't live with it anymore. My TikTok feed at the time would also not shut up about ice baths. And yes, I'm on TikTok. I'm going through a midlife crisis, not skipping pop culture. So after the 50th ice bath video or so, I decided I wanted to try it. Dip my toes into this whole ice-bathing thing.

My search for a container large enough for my chubby body and some ice water began.

II. Understanding the Mid-life Crisis

This isn't another one of those self-help books claiming to have all the answers to your oh-so-unique mid-life crisis. But explaining mine might help you figure out yours. So at the end of the day, maybe it is. I guess we'll find out together.

First, you may ask, what is a mid-life crisis and am I having one?

A mid-life crisis is, in essence, a period of transition - a time when you look back on your life and question whether it's been everything you hoped it would be. It's a time of self-reflection, introspection, and, of course, a dash of good old-fashioned shock and panic. After all, nothing spices up life like the sudden realization that you're halfway through. Even writing that sends a bit of a shockwave through my spine.

Some psychologists argue that the mid-life crisis is a normal and healthy part of human development. It's a time to reevaluate your priorities, make necessary adjustments, and ultimately emerge as a wiser, more self-aware individual. Sounds like a real blast, doesn't it?

Others, however, believe that the mid-life crisis is just a convenient excuse for acting out and making poor decisions. Because, you know, everyone needs a scapegoat for their circus of chaos.

Whatever your take on the matter, one thing is clear: the mid-life crisis is as inevitable as death, taxes, and that sinking feeling that you've left the stove on. So why not embrace it with open arms? After all, laughter is the best medicine - even if the joke's on you.

Also, if you can't take a joke and you're one of those old grumpy mid-life crisis-ers, this book probably isn't for you. Here at Cold Feat, we wear a smile throughout our mid-life crisis.

Weeeeeeeee!

Grab your bathing suit (or not) and let's dive right into the icy depths of this thing called a mid-life crisis. You know, because most of us, including me, are completely clueless about what's happening.

III. The Unexpected Arrival of a Mid-Life Crisis

If you're reading this, chances are you've either put things together and realized that you are indeed in the throws of a mid-life crisis orrrrrrrr... you've tried all the conventional solutions: the sports cars, the wild adventures, the impulsive haircuts, the *gasp* tattoos (don't look at me, I've had these for years). And they were about as effective as a screen door on a submarine. But don't worry, I'm here to tell you that there's a whole world beyond those tired, overused stereotypes. Because nothing screams "originality" quite like a self-help book dripping with sarcasm.

Writing that, I don't even know if I'm kidding or not. Are there a lot of self-help books dripping with sarcasm? Should I be doing more market research? Meh, I'm busy writing and cold bathing and breathing and working and hanging out with my kid and... you get it.

Here's the thing with a mid-life crisis that they don't tell you about. They being, anyone. They. come. out. of. NO. WHERE. As you read above, mine came from a photo at the DMV. You're just doing your best and BOOM, your psyche gets punched in the nose.

To say that it's shocking is an understatement.

IV. Why Shock Is A Natural First Response

In the world of psychology, shock is akin to the underappreciated hero in a blockbuster movie, always making its dramatic entrance right when you're facing the villain. And what a show it puts on during a mid-life crisis! The once-clear waters of your life's path are now as murky as a coffee aficionado's espresso shot, and shock is the unwanted barista serving it up.

Speaking of clear waters, let's add a twist to this thrilling tale of crises - ice bathing. Imagine shock as a surprise plunge into a tub full of icy cold water. It's intense, it's unpleasant, but boy does it wake you up! Your body reacts immediately, heart pounding, breath hitching, nerves firing – a visceral testament to your survival instincts.

In the context of a mid-life crisis, the initial shock is like that ice bath. The cold realization that you've reached a point of dissatisfaction with your life is jarring. You're suddenly shivering in the frosty air of discontent, and much like an ice bath, it's uncomfortable, it's chilling, but it can also be remarkably clarifying.

So next time you feel the shock of your mid-life crisis hitting, take a deep breath, embrace the chill, and remember: This shock might be the wake-up call you need to fix it all. What I'm saying is that shock isn't necessarily a bad first response, it's what you do next that's important.

V. Navigating Through the Shock

Okay, now that you've been shocked, how do you navigate through it? Well, your humble author - yes, yours truly - knows a thing or two about navigating through the shock of a mid-life crisis. Picture me, happily trotting along on the highway of life, moving halfway around the world, getting a job in a foreign country, and out of absolutely nowhere find myself veering off into the dirt path marked "Mid-Life Crisis Avenue." The initial shock was more of a dull game of Clue. Who dun it? How did we get here? It was super confusing because before seeing that faithful picture taken by the young man at not the DMV, I didn't know it was happening.

I guess you can say my shock was more of a dull, how the hell did I not notice that I was in a mid-life crisis instead of an oh my god, I'm IN a mid-life crisis.

Anywho… I just came up with the A, B, and C's of mid-life crisis and how to navigate them. I think it makes sense for everyone, but you tell me.

Are you ready?

- **A**cknowledge: Like a surprise house guest, shock cannot be ignored. Give it a nod, offer it a cup of green tea, but don't let it take over your entire house. If something feels off, pretending that it's not happening is not going to make you feel better, it will make you feel worse. Or it will make the bad part of the mid-life crisis last much longer.

- **B**reathe: Seems basic, right? But when you're in the throes of a shock response, your body tends to forget about this little thing called oxygen. Deep, conscious breathing can remind your body and mind that you are, in fact, still alive and capable of dealing with this. You're going to need this later when we talk about getting in that chilly water. Speaking of, on my right wrist I have an Apple Ultra watch (yes, it's worth the moola), and on my left is a rubber bracelet that I made on Amazon that says BREATHE. It's a good reminder to do so in stressful situations.

- **C**ommunicate: With friends, family, or a trusted therapist. Don't bottle up your feelings like they're a rare vintage wine to be savored later. Spoiler alert:

they're not. Let people be there for you, rather than going on the whole thing alone. You'll be thankful they're with you. And yes, I know this is harder done than said, but hear me out.

Now, let me pass on some general advice, a life jacket of sorts, to help you manage the shock and process your feelings. Some of this is going to feel weird and I'm okay with that. Unlike above, it doesn't have a cool mnemonic, it's just a bunch of thoughts:

- Pause and Reflect: Don't rush into drastic changes or make impulsive decisions. You're not trying to beat a world record in crisis resolution. Take your time to evaluate your life and identify what's causing your discomfort. For me, it was physical pain and body weight. I reflected quickly, but I think it all worked out because I'm here writing this book.

- Reframe Your Thoughts: The mid-life crisis, for all its notorious reputation, is not the end of the world! Think of it as a new beginning, a chance to rewrite your story. After all, every good story needs a twist, right? Consider this an opportunity, not a punishment. Fix your shit, don't dwell on it.

- Take Care of Your Body: As I said, for me, this was my core issue. But even if it's not yours, it's important. Regular exercise, a healthy diet, and sufficient sleep can help reduce stress and increase resilience. Sleep. Get more sleep!

- Find Joy: Engage in activities you love or try new hobbies. Rediscovering passion can ease the tension and offer new perspectives on life. We forget that choosing happiness is an option. No, really.

Remember, a mid-life crisis is an opportunity. It's your chance to reflect, reassess, and, if necessary, redefine your life. And with this handy guide, you are now equipped to sail through the shock and emerge on the other side, a little wiser, a little stronger, and hopefully, a lot happier.

VI. Grounding Exercises

Okay, for those of you who have never tried this sort of thing, it's going to be SUPER weird, but trust Papa Donnelly. You're safe.

Grounding is a technique that can help steady your brain and bring you back to a state of mental equilibrium. These exercises can be a lifesaver when you're caught in the whirlwind of a shock response. They work like an anchor, tethering your mind to the present and preventing it from spiraling into the abyss of panic and confusion. So, without further ado, let's walk through 3 easy-to-follow grounding exercises you can do from literally anywhere.

1. The 5-4-3-2-1 Technique

This exercise can help bring your focus back to the present by using your five senses. Once you're comfortable and have your breathing under control, here's how to do it:

- Focus on 5 things you can see around you. Perhaps it's a family photo, your favorite mug, or the color of your walls. Super simple, just see them.

- Find 4 things you can touch. It might be the feel of your clothing, the smooth surface of a table, or the texture of a nearby object.

- Acknowledge 3 things you can hear. This could be the sound of your own breath, birds chirping outside, or distant traffic noises.

- Think about 2 things you can smell. Maybe you can smell your own perfume, the aroma of your coffee, or the scent of a nearby flower.

- Seek out 1 thing you can taste. This could be the aftertaste of your recent meal, a sip of water, or even the taste of your own mouth.

2. Grounding Meditation

This is a calming exercise that can help reconnect you with your body and the physical world around you. Here's a simple process:

- Sit or lie down comfortably in a quiet place. Close your eyes if you wish.

- Take a few slow, deep breaths. With each inhale, envision calm energy entering your body and with each exhale, imagine stress and shock leaving your body.

- Now, mentally scan your body from your toes to your head. Notice any tension or discomfort, but don't try to change anything.

- Visualize a grounding cord going from your body deep into the earth. Imagine it anchoring you securely to the ground.

- Remain in this state for as long as you need, letting the feeling of being anchored to the earth fill you with a sense of stability and calm.

3. Progressive Muscle Relaxation

This technique helps you to focus on the sensation of relaxation and can be particularly effective for those who are more kinesthetic. Here's a quick guide:

- Find a quiet place to sit or lie down comfortably.

- Start with your toes. Tense them as hard as you can for about 5 seconds, and then release the tension. Notice the sensation of relaxation.

- Gradually work your way up through different muscle groups - your legs, stomach, hands, arms, shoulders, neck, and face - repeating the tension and release process.

- By the time you reach the top of your head, your entire body should feel relaxed. Take a moment to enjoy this state of physical calm.

Remember, the goal of grounding exercises is to refocus your attention on the here and now. These exercises aren't an escape from the shock of a mid-life crisis, but a way to steady yourself as you navigate its choppy waters. So, go on, give them a try, and find your way back to solid ground.

VII. Summary

So far you've heard a little bit about who I am, that I take ice baths, that I was having a mid-life crisis and a few of the ways I worked through what I was feeling.

In the next chapter, we'll tackle our dirty mistress, denial. Ah, denial! We'll dive into the psychology behind denial, why it's a common reaction to a mid-life crisis and strategies to work through it. As we've learned, it's crucial to face our feelings head-on rather than ignore them, and denial can be a significant roadblock on the journey to acceptance and resolution.

So, brace yourselves we're about to get real weird and dive into the human psyche in our ongoing journey through mid-life crises. Let's continue unraveling the complexities of these life transitions and their psychological impacts together. Stay tuned for more insights, advice, and perhaps a little bit of humor to lighten the mood, because who said navigating a mid-life crisis couldn't be enlightening and entertaining?

Chapter 2: Denial

"The Art of Ignoring an Elephant in the Room"

I. Introduction (The memoir part)

What's the joke about denial? Something about it not being a river, right? Well, mine was a very big river and it was flowing through every day of my life. That being said, for a very long time, I was denying even having denial.

It's funny, but humans have this incredible capability to ignore or forget almost anything. When I first thought about writing this chapter, I immediately knew what I was going to write about, but only remembered it because I forced myself to.

In 2012, I moved to Brooklyn, New York. It's odd, in 2003 I moved thousands of miles from home to Mesa, Arizona, but the gravity of moving to New York, just two hundred miles north from where I lived seemed so much further.

In Pennsylvania, I'd been a college recruiter for a few years, and an adjunct professor for a year or two. I was doing well for myself with a house and a big, beautiful, red Ford F150 that sounded like a beast every time I started her up. Yes, she was a girl.

Moving to New York, I sold everything I owned, my house, even my records. I still think about a few rares that I included in a bulk sale. This Japanese print of a Johnny Cash album particularly stands out. Anyway, this story is really about a particular commute in New York.

On the train, a homeless man was rubbing himself on the other side of the aisle and kept making eye contact with me. After moving to another train, two men got into a fistfight. After leaving the train and walking toward my office, an old man was completely naked right on Park Ave looking in the trash, and yet another man was dressed up in a pink cowboy outfit, and skirt, and completely painted in makeup.

By the time I got my coffee and got to the office the visuals that I'd seen that morning disappeared and I started writing ads.

New York had that kind of insanity to it often. You'd see the most heartbreaking, beautiful, sad, destructive, whatever, and then you'd go about your day. This also reminds me to tell everyone that doesn't live in New York that they're nice people! They're just busy and your questions are most likely slowing them down to get somewhere important (or more comfortable).

Anyway, the story above brings me to my mid-life crisis and how easily we can forget if not completely ignore things right in front of our faces.

Every day I'd see myself getting tired walking with Jameson. I'd see my reflection in windows and tell myself, with a straight face, that it was the curvature of the glass that made me look like that. "That's not you being overweight Jason, it's the mirror, reflecting strangely…" Do you understand how powerful your brain has to be to not only make that kind of shit up but believe it?

The next paragraph might be the most important in the book, pay attention. Write it down. Highlight it.

We allow ourselves to be whatever we want and that goes both ways. We allow ourselves to tell these lies and believe them or we allow ourselves to fix the things that cause us to have to lie to ourselves (which is much harder).

You can argue with me about this until you're blue in the face, but unfortunately, this is a book and I can't hear you.

II. The Psychology of Denial

Life is packed with more curves and loop-de-loops than Hershey Park (I actually worked there for two summers, one as a ride operator and one as an entertainer, juggling for the Trash Time Band, but this isn't the memoir part so let's move on). Along for the ride is our good friend, denial. Often acting like that person at a party who overstays their welcome, denial swoops in to "save the day," but usually just ends up stealing the snacks and hogging the sofa.

Denial, that psychological party-crasher, is essentially our brain's clumsy attempt at a magic trick. "Look over there! Nothing to see here," it says, as it sweeps the uncomfortable truths under the rug. It's our mind's built-in filter that conveniently blurs out all the bits of reality that seem too scary, too overwhelming, or just too darn inconvenient to deal with. It's a self-inflicted safety measure, but logically, it might not feel like that at all.

When you're standing on the precipice of a life-altering event, like, let's say, losing a job, your brain might resort to this trusty trick. "Job loss? Nope, didn't see that coming. This must be a prank!" Denial steps in like an overzealous security guard, ready to fend off the painful blow.

Denial is a product of a heated rivalry in our mental family: the ego and the id. Picture them as squabbling siblings. The ego is the responsible older brother, attempting to negotiate between the wild desires of the younger sibling, the id, and the stern voice of reality. Sometimes the ego lets id get away with a little bit too much and that's when denial comes into play, a convenient blindfold to hide the unpleasant reality.

But like an overstuffed closet, eventually, reality will tumble out, generally at the most inconvenient time. Denial may feel like a cozy blanket on a cold night, but eventually, you have to get out of bed.

Mid-Life Crisis: When Denial Decides to Move In

Mid-life, that grand ol' stage of life when you're supposed to have it all figured out, often turns out to be more of a crisis than a comfort. And denial, sensing an opportunity, packs its bags and moves in.

People tend to hit the 'mid-life crisis' period, look around, and think, "Wait, this isn't what I signed up for!" They feel out of place, disoriented, and if they're really lucky, they get to have a full-blown existential crisis. This is the perfect time for denial to step in and say, "Hey, you're not lost! This is just the scenic route."

When we're grappling with the reality that we've reached the midpoint of our life and may not have accomplished what we hoped, denial can seem like a pretty attractive option. It's easier to stick our heads in the sand and pretend we're still those carefree 20-year-olds with the world at our fingertips, rather than deal with the reality of receding hairlines, expanding waistlines, and dreams that seem to be playing an intense game of hard-to-get.

Remember, though, that denial has an incredible knack for overstaying its welcome. It may offer a temporary escape from mid-life turmoil, but eventually, you're going to have to come back from that scenic route and face the music.

So let's not give denial the master key to our minds. It's high time we demoted it from a permanent lodger to a fleeting visitor, one who pops by for a cup of green tea and then is gently, but firmly, shown the door.

III. Signs of Denial During a Mid-life Crisis

If life is a jigsaw puzzle, the mid-life crisis is the sneaky piece that looks like it should fit but doesn't. It's that unpredictable storm in the middle of what should be a leisurely sail through life. And as we discussed in the previous section, denial, that uninvited guest, often pops up during this time like a pesky game of whack-a-mole. But how can you spot this crafty character in your thought patterns and behaviors? Put on your Sherlock Holmes cap, because we're going on a denial-detection mission.

The Red Flags of Denial

First off, denial is a master of disguise. It can take many forms and blend into your daily thought patterns and behaviors so smoothly that you'd swear it was always a part of the script. Here are some common ways that denial might be trying to sneak in through the stage door:

- Excessive Nostalgia: There's nothing wrong with a little trip down memory lane now and then. But if you're spending more time reminiscing about your glory days than actually living in the present, it might be denial, decked out in sepia tones, trying to convince you that the past is better than the present.

- Drastic Changes in Appearance: Is your wardrobe suddenly bursting with clothes that would be more suitable for a college party than a parent-teacher conference? Are you contemplating tattoos, piercings, or flashy sports cars? Denial might be trying to convince you that if you look like your 20-year-old self, you can feel like them too.

- Frustration and Impatience: If your fuse is shorter than a goldfish's attention span and everything seems to be irritating you more than usual, denial may be lurking in the wings. It's much easier to lash out at the world than face internal chaos, isn't it?

- Risk-taking Behavior: If you're suddenly engaging in risky activities or making impulsive decisions, check the backseat. Denial might be on board, telling you that these adrenaline-pumping activities will mask the uncomfortable feelings you're dealing with.

- Fantasies of Escaping: If you're constantly daydreaming about leaving it all behind for a life on a tropical island or a cabin in the woods, you might have a stowaway. Denial loves to convince us that running away from our problems is a viable solution.

- Ignoring Aging: Ignoring doctor's appointments, refusing to accept physical limitations, or joking excessively about being "old" might seem like harmless behavior. But that might be denial in disguise, putting up a smokescreen between you and the reality of aging.

So, now that we've got the wanted poster, spotting the crafty culprit will hopefully become a bit easier. Remember, acknowledging that denial is at play is half the battle. The next half is giving it the boot and dealing with your mid-life changes head-on, with your chin up, a brave smile, and perhaps a glass of really good boxed wine (or in a bottle, whatever).

Because at the end of the day, mid-life isn't a crisis, it's just another challenge—and by now, we all know we're pretty good at those, don't we? So, get out there, and show that crisis who's boss!

IV. Why Denial Doesn't Work

We've all heard the old saying, "What you don't know can't hurt you," right? But in reality, that's about as accurate as claiming chocolate is a vegetable because it comes from a bean. As we navigate the roller coaster ride of a mid-life crisis, denial might feel like a painkiller, numbing the discomfort. But just like a painkiller doesn't cure the disease, denial doesn't resolve the underlying issues—it merely masks them. Let's dive into why denial can be a harmful strategy and explore some real-life examples. The Perils of Ignorance

Let's say someone loses their job, but instead of doing something about it, he chooses denial as his coping mechanism. He pretends that everything's hunky-dory, avoids discussing his job loss, and spends his days in his pajamas, binging on Netflix and popcorn. While it might bring temporary comfort, in the long run, this denial prevents him from facing the reality of his situation and taking steps to find a new job.

Psychologists call this 'maladaptive coping.' It's like putting a Band-Aid on a wound that needs stitches; it might stop the bleeding for a bit, but it won't facilitate proper healing. Denial, particularly in a mid-life crisis, can lead to harmful behaviors.

A Tale of Two Denials

Let's consider two real-life examples: Tom and Jerry (not the cartoon characters, mind you). Both are experiencing a mid-life crisis. Tom chooses denial as his sidekick. He ignores his feelings of dissatisfaction, splurges on a fast motorcycle, and starts partying like there's no tomorrow, trying to recapture his youth. He's avoiding his doctor's appointments and neglecting his responsibilities.

On the other hand, Jerry decides to face his mid-life crisis head-on. He recognizes his feelings, seeks guidance from a therapist, and starts investing time in meaningful hobbies. He's staying physically active and taking care of his health. Fast-forward a few years, and the difference is glaring. Tom's denial has led him to a lifestyle that's impacting his health and relationships negatively. The motorcycle was fun for a while, but the novelty has worn off, and the underlying issues remain unresolved.

Jerry, meanwhile, is healthier, more content, and has a newfound passion for painting. He's navigated the storm and emerged stronger.

V. From Denial to Understanding

So, you've been sailing the choppy seas of a mid-life crisis with denial as your trusty first mate. It's offered you comfort, distraction, and possibly a collection of leather jackets. But as we've discussed, denial is a fair-weather friend, ready to abandon ship at the first sight of an iceberg. It's high time we traded this sneaky stowaway for a more reliable companion: understanding.

From Shallow Distractions to Understanding

Picture this: you're standing on a beach, trying to hold back the waves. That's denial. Now imagine turning around, diving in, and swimming with the current. That's understanding.

Understanding is the act of recognizing and embracing your reality. It doesn't mean giving up or being passive. Instead, it's about acknowledging where you are, what you're feeling, and then deciding where you want to go from there. In the context of a mid-life crisis, understanding allows you to address your feelings of discomfort, dissatisfaction, or regret and use them as catalysts for positive change.

Upgrading Your Coping Mechanisms

So, how do we make this trade-off from denial to understanding? Here are some strategies:

- Practice Mindfulness: Mindfulness is all about being in the present moment without judgment. Instead of dwelling on past glories or future uncertainties, focus on the here and now. Take up practices like meditation, yoga, breathwork, or even ice bathing (don't worry we'll get to it). They help create a mental space where you can observe your thoughts and feelings without feeling overwhelmed.

- Seek Professional Help: Therapists and counselors are like tour guides for your psyche. They can help you navigate through your feelings and eventually accept them. Even having this book is a good step in the right direction.

- Stay Connected: Don't isolate yourself. Keep the channels of communication open with your loved ones. Speak about your fears, anxieties, and thoughts. You'll often find that you're not alone, and shared experiences can lead to greater understanding.

- Channel Your Energy: Find healthy outlets for your emotions. This could be anything from painting, gardening, or writing, to running, cycling, or dancing. Engaging in activities that you love can help you accept the changes in your life.

- Reevaluate and Set New Goals: This can be an excellent time to evaluate your life goals. What have you achieved? What remains? Set new goals aligned with your current aspirations, values, and circumstances.

The Benefits of Understanding

So, what does upgrading your mid-life crisis management toolbox from denial to understanding bring you?

- Peace and Contentment: The constant internal struggle of denying reality is tiring (even if you don't realize it). When you understand, you permit yourself to be at peace with your current state.

- Better Decision Making: With understanding, you see things as they are, not clouded by fear or wishful thinking. This clarity paves the way for better, more informed decisions.

- Improved Relationships: Denial can put a strain on your relationships as you may tend to withdraw or behave out of character. Understanding allows open, honest communication and fosters stronger bonds.

- Personal Growth: Understanding is the first step towards personal growth and self-improvement. Once you acknowledge your reality, you can work on changing or improving it.

Remember, while denial might seem like an attractive tourist destination, understanding is where you set up a home. It's comfortable, welcoming, and although it takes work to maintain, the benefits are worth the effort. So, as we continue our mid-life journey, let's pack our bags with understanding and a good dose of optimism. After all, life is all about growing, changing, and moving forward—one understanding-filled step at a time.

VI. Summary

Denial only provides a temporary escape from reality, causing further complications when reality eventually surfaces. This aspect of denial becomes particularly prevalent during a mid-life crisis, where people may find their life's reality vastly different from their expectations. While denial might offer a temporary distraction from these issues, it's crucial to acknowledge it as a temporary visitor and face the realities of life.

Above we've outlined various red flags of denial, but as I'm pretty sure we all know, a lot of us completely skip red flags. We think about something else or just completely ignore them. It's important to be present and think about what you feel.

In the next chapter, we'll dive into some painful stuff, and just to make sure there are no surprises, it's the chapter I talk about losing my mother-in-law. And it's called pain for a reason.

Chapter 3: Pain

The Thorny Path of Loss and Grief

I. Introduction (The memoir part)

I already said, "Fuck cancer," right? Okay, I want that to be very clear.

Should I say it again?

FUCK. period. CANCER. period.

Okay, it still doesn't have the gravitas I was looking for, but it is what it is.

In the months before Kirsten passed, I kept getting these ice bath videos popping up in my feeds and I thought to myself how much I hated the cold.

I told myself repeatedly, "I could never do that."

I also have a problem with anyone telling me that I can't do something, including myself. So I did some research and started reading about just how many benefits cold water had for the dippers.

The most interesting piece was about happiness. There's been research done that shows that submerging your body in cold water increases dopamine concentration by 250%. Most people know that dopamine is responsible for happiness in a lot of ways, but the other things it's responsible for are allowing you to feel pleasure, satisfaction, and motivation.

If you feel good about something, it's most likely because of a surge of dopamine in your brain. Cold bathing is basically cocaine, except it lasts longer. And I can only assume what you're asking yourself is, "We sure are talking a lot about cocaine instead about your mother-in-law. Did you forget?"

I did not.

Let's do this.

One of the first things that Kirsten said to me when we met was how soft my hands were. I am 99.9% positive that she said this out of kindness and my hands were soft, I'm a writer who sits at a desk and types all day, how rough could they be?

That being said, there is a 0.1% chance that she said it to make me question everything. Does she think I'M soft? Here comes Jason and his dainty hands made of silk. What are you going to do with those hands, Jason? Pet a kitten?

Possibly.

Where was I? Oh, right. She had such a way with things. She was a mom's mom who oozed empathy. She cared with every ounce of her body and when she cared about something you could physically feel it.

I can still hear her coming into the house and saying, "Hello helloooo," in an almost Mrs. Doubtfire voice, announcing herself. I find myself doing it now to remind myself of her and how much I miss her.

For years, we knew that we were going to lose Kirsten. It wasn't the fun cancer that comes over, brings drinks, and then goes home. It was the cancer that took over every quiet lull in conversations. The one where you forget about it, but then don't, and sadness creeps into an otherwise happy day.

She would do chemo, implement routines and regimens, and eat things that would help, but at the end of the day, we all knew it was hiding just on the blurry outskirts of our vision.

I'm almost positive that the reason Kirsten lasted so long was because of a little boy named Jameson. My son. I'm sitting here crying typing this, but gonna talk directly to my son quickly.

It's all you, Jameson. Mormor loved you with her whole heart, buddy. When you're older and you read this, take a look at the pictures hanging around the house, she'll always be here, forever, no matter what... She gave the kind of love you take with you forever.

Okay, back to the book. Simply said, I knew that I was going to be crushed losing Kirsten and honestly, I wanted anything that could help me through it. It's a weird feeling preparing so long for pain. You can brace before you fall, but when it's years or even months of waiting, it's a different kind of bracing.

In walks ice cold water...

Who knew that subjecting myself to freezing temperatures could be the secret to coming to terms with loss? I guess I kinda did, that's why I started. But yeah, buckle up, dear reader, because we're about to dive into the frosty intersection of grief and ice bathing.

Is ice bathing art or the social media that comes with it? Maybe if you make your own tub? Have you seen my swimming trunks, they're Cold Feat originals... I've derailed.

How Freezing My Buns Off Helped Me Cope

My mother-in-law's battle with cancer ended on March 16th, leaving behind a gaping void that will never be filled. Amidst the chaos, 42 days prior, I started jumping in the water, every single morning. I can still hear her telling me that I was crazy and lovingly following up that I was a real Viking (even though she was a Dane with Viking roots).

Even writing this I'm tearing up thinking about her. She really was magic. I wish that everyone out there has their own Kirsten. My life trajectory will always be better because of her in my life.

II. The Bitter Pill of Grief

Now, how does one confront the cruel, unrelenting nature of existence other than by dunking themselves in a tub of ice water? I don't know, because I chose column A. You may be thinking, "There's gotta be some other, less torturous ways of processing grief." And to that, I say: "Why settle for conventional methods when you can confuse the living hell out of your body?"

Nothing puts the human experience into perspective quite like the sensation of turning into a human popsicle.

Each and every dip made me realize that you can't be in emotional pain in ice water. I know, I know, you're saying that if you're in enough pain, you can, but I'll be the first to tell you that cold water does something to your system. It doesn't necessarily take away the pain, but it moves it to the side while your body tries to keep itself alive.

True story, or... I guess, true science, when you enter cold water, your body undergoes physiological changes in response to the sudden temperature shift. Here's a quick breakdown of the process:

- Cold Shock Response: This is the first reaction when your body is immersed in cold water. The skin's sudden exposure to cold temperatures causes a set of cardiovascular reflexes, leading to an initial gasp for air, hyperventilation (you can see this in my first ice bath video), elevated heart rate, and higher blood pressure. This reaction can cause panic and disorientation, and in extreme cases, it may even lead to cardiac arrest, especially in individuals with pre-existing heart conditions.

- Thermal Gradient Change: As the body starts cooling down, the thermal gradient (difference in temperature between the body core and the environment) causes heat to flow out from the body, reducing the skin and muscle temperature.

- Peripheral Vasoconstriction: Do I sound smart yet? Don't worry, I looked it up. The body attempts to conserve heat by narrowing blood vessels in the skin and extremities, a process called vasoconstriction. This action reduces the amount of blood flowing to these areas, minimizing heat loss from the surface of the body. It also directs warm blood to the vital organs in the body's core to maintain their function. AKA keep you alive.

- Muscle Cooling and Reduced Dexterity: Cooling of the muscles can lead to reduced strength and fine motor control, particularly in the hands. This can impair your ability to swim or perform rescue actions like grabbing onto a life ring.

- Shivering and Non-shivering Thermogenesis: Shivering is an involuntary muscle contraction mechanism to generate heat. Non-shivering thermogenesis, on the other hand, involves the metabolism of brown adipose tissue (brown fat) to produce heat.

- Hypothermia: If you remain in cold water for a prolonged period, your body's core temperature may drop significantly, leading to hypothermia. Symptoms include intense shivering, confusion, weak pulse, slow and shallow breathing, loss of coordination, and in severe cases, unconsciousness or death.

- Immersion Diuresis: Immersion in cold water also causes the body to increase urine output. The peripheral vasoconstriction pushes more blood toward the core, which the body interprets as fluid overload. As a result, it increases urine production to balance the perceived overload. I often feel like I have to pee after I just peed when I get in.

- Cold-Induced Vasodilation (CIVD): After an initial phase of vasoconstriction, some areas, such as fingers and toes, may experience cycles of vasodilation where the blood vessels open up. This is a protective mechanism to prevent local frostbite.

So, as fun as all of these sound, it's almost impossible to focus on your sad feelings. Your body is too worried about getting the blood out of your extremities and to your core to keep you alive.

That being said, it's also important to note that individual responses to cold water can vary depending on factors like body composition, acclimatization to cold, age, and overall health status. Some people may be more susceptible to cold shock, hypothermia, and other dangers of cold water exposure.

For myself, I've tested cold dips for up to 10 minutes, and even after two hundred plunges, 10 minutes makes parts of me hurt too much to enjoy. So yes, you can have too much of a good thing.

This section needs to have an added disclaimer. Yes, ice water will make you not think of pretty much anything, for a short time, but after you're out, you still have to process. Always remember that. It's not about deleting the sadness, it's about controlling it and working through it.

III. The Ritual of Pain During a Mid-life Crisis

Every day. No matter what. I got in the water.

In the weeks that followed my mother-in-law's passing, I committed even stronger to a daily ice bath ritual. Every morning, I would lower myself into my tub's frosty embrace. And as the chill seeped into my bones, I found that it forced me to take a minute (or five) to myself. It's extremely difficult to think about very much when you're in water that is often below freezing (I used pounds of Epsom salt to make the water even more difficult to freeze).

Each shiver and gasp became a reminder of the fragility of life and the importance of acknowledging and honoring the pain that accompanies loss. Sure, it was a bit masochistic, but sometimes you need to get a little creative to make sense of the incomprehensible.

I'm writing this section on a train to Holstebro, Denmark. We just passed Odense. At 4:30 am this morning before I left, I jumped in my chest freezer, as one does before an overnight work trip. It was a hard time getting in today and in my social media post I said, "It doesn't get easier, it just gets to be a part of your routine." I think that's something that people need to understand.

I don't think there's been a day (that the water was below 4 degrees) that I got in and was happy about the feeling. Yes, some days are easier to get in, for one reason or another, but it's never an enjoyable experience. Like I've said before, the best part about cold baths is getting out. As the title suggests, it's a ritual in pain, and the healing comes after that delightful dopamine release. Getting out of the water is a release that lasts for hours.

That being said, it also has just a few other scientifically proven benefits:

- Reduced Muscle Inflammation and Soreness: Many athletes use cold water immersion or ice baths after intense workouts to help reduce inflammation and muscle soreness. The cold helps narrow the blood vessels and decreases metabolic activity, which reduces swelling and tissue breakdown.

- Improved Circulation: When your body is exposed to cold, it responds by narrowing (constricting) your blood vessels in the periphery of your body and shunting the blood to your core to maintain your body temperature. This movement of blood can improve your circulation.

- Enhanced Mood: Cold water immersion can stimulate the production of endorphins, the body's natural painkillers, and mood elevators. It can also increase the production of norepinephrine in the brain, which could have an antidepressant effect.

- Increased Alertness: The shock of the cold water can result in increased oxygen intake and an accelerated heart rate, which can lead to a natural state of alertness and increased energy.

- Boosted Immune Response: Some studies suggest that regular exposure to cold water can boost the immune system by increasing the number of white blood cells in the body. *More research is needed in this area to fully understand the potential benefits.

- Improved Skin and Hair Health: Cold water can help tighten the skin and pores, which may reduce the likelihood of getting clogged pores. Similarly, it can make hair appear shinier and healthier by tightening cuticles and follicles.

- Potential Metabolism Boost: There is some evidence to suggest that cold water immersion can stimulate brown fat production, a type of fat that burns energy to generate body heat. This can potentially boost metabolism and aid in weight loss. *Again, more research is needed to confirm these effects.

- Mental Fortitude: This one is the most powerful for me and has been proven in my own studies. After a few weeks of doing it, you are stronger mentally than you've ever been. There's something insanely powerful about forcing a body that does not want to do something to do it anyway. Which sounds way worse than cold bathing, but you get it.

All these benefits are great, but I gotta say it, I would rather have Kirsten back instead, unfortunately, I was not given a choice.

IV. Coping with Pain

As my daily ice bath practice continued, I found that the ritual provided a space for me to truly feel and process the pain that accompanied Kirsten's passing.

In those frozen moments, I discovered that sometimes the only way to make sense of grief is to lean into the discomfort, to allow yourself to truly feel the loss, and to emerge from the experience with a newfound appreciation for life's fleeting nature.

The time in the ice allowed the pain to go away so I could just be in the feeling. It's an odd thing to explain, taking away the pain to feel the pain? Because that's what it is. Thinking about Kirsten at any point makes my eyes well up with tears, but in the water, I could focus on the thoughts behind it without the emotion getting in the way.

So, there you have it: a heartwarming (or, perhaps more accurately, heart-freezing) tale of loss, love, and the unlikely solace of ice baths. It may not be the most conventional approach, but as the old saying goes, "When life gives you ice, throw your chunky, depressed, aging body into a tub of it." Or something like that.

Kirsten, you're missed every single day. Thanks for being a part of my life.

V. Summary

In this section we talk about my hatred of cancer (fuck you cancer), my mother-in-law's battle, and the impending loss that loomed over us all. How in the middle of it all, I stumbled upon the idea of ice baths, as a means to cope with it. Over the months I discovered that immersing my body in freezing temperatures triggered physiological responses that shifted my focus away from the pain and grief. I reflected on Kirsten's love and the impact she had on my life.

In the second section, we explored the concept of using ice baths as a tool for processing grief. Throughout this part I spoke about the physical effects of cold water immersion, highlighting the body's adaptive responses and the distracting nature of the experience. I shared a few personal experiences with daily ice baths and emphasized that while it doesn't eliminate pain, it helps momentarily set it aside.

In the next section, we'll talk about the complex process of bargaining in the face of grief. Stay tuned as we start navigating the challenging terrain of bargaining and share some insights on finding a balance between longing for what is lost and embracing the present moment.

Chapter 4: Bargaining

Desperate Deals with Life

I. Introduction (The memoir part)

Two weeks after Kirsten left us, I received my last present from her. A birthday present she was so worried about getting me before she couldn't. It was a two-day breathwork masterclass led by Tim van der Vliet and Birger Hanzen (both contributors to this book in chapter 11).

Before going into it, I'd only done one other breathing exercise. I did it at my work desk, watching a video by that guy I said I wouldn't mention again, and did 30 deep breaths and held them. From this single breathing exercise, I realized that breathing could change my inner workings. My heart rate elevated. I started to sweat. I felt like I was working out, but sitting still.

I was definitely not a masterclass-ready breathworker, but I needed more.

The class was over the weekend of April 15th and 16th. I'd only been ice bathing for a little over 2 ½ months but ice bathing every day like I was gives you the mindset that you can do anything.

I took a cab to the Hillerød station, then a train to Copenhagen, and walked from the Kastrup station over to TarGet Power Gym. I was told that this gym is where some of the biggest powerlifters in Denmark trained.

Other than doing a bunch of cold baths, I was out of my element, to say the least. The class promised to teach us how to breathe calm into our daily lives, get better focus, develop body intelligence, and release stress. It also had an interesting line on the flyer that said, "Get high on your own supply. Power your own DMT release." But after reading it, I thought it was crazy to think that it was possible.

If you aren't familiar, DMT is a powerful psychedelic drug, with serotonergic effects on the human brain, which can induce a rapid and intense psychedelic experience. It's also found in a lot of plants and animals, including humans. So, releasing it could be possible, but to me, unlikely.

That being said, the guys said that they would teach us how to release essential neurotransmitters like dopamine, endorphins, and serotonin to increase our sports performance. The dozen or so of us in the class were all ears. And they went through the science behind breathing, oxygenating blood, and an incredible technique called Tummo breathing, where you create an inner fire and through breathwork, possibly release DMT.

Guess who did it?

That's right, your boy, Jason.

After 45 minutes of Tummo breathing, multiple rounds, I looked up to the ceiling, and out of nowhere, it changed from white to green. I tried stopping it, shaking my head, and turning it back to white. Then I realized what was happening. I dove back in, I let go, and I watched it turn back to green. The green slipped into the canopy of a jungle. The wind blew through the trees and I could see them moving together. The music Tim was playing was called, "Om Mani Padme Hum 1" by Jane Winther (you can find it on Spotify).

It felt like a tribal village, connected, ancient, and in tune with everyone. I could see their culture and the love they were pushing into the world. It gave me goosebumps then and now writing about it. I opened my eyes realizing that I did this through breathing. Just. Breathing.

Then I tested more of their theories.

May 10th, 2023

In the masterclass above they taught me about how oxygenating the blood before any strenuous activity would allow you to do that activity at a higher level. Ironically, I was listening to the chapters on the exact subject in Scott Carney's book, What Doesn't Kill Us, during my test.

If you're looking for a killer book on breathing, cold exposure, and a lot of other brilliant things, go pick it up after you're done with this one. His is much more brainy than yours truly.

Anyway, in Hillerød, there's a big loop around our smaller town of Tulstrup. The loop is a little over 2 kilometers and I planned to walk around the loop once while breathing like I was running. Oxygenating my blood as much as possible before taking a jog back around.

*Please test the theory yourself to see just how difficult it is to breathe deeply through your nose and out your mouth while taking a simple walk. It's weird and harder than you ever expect.

Rounding the loop, I noticed that I was right around 1.9 km on my walk, so I walked into a field near the end, turned around at about 1.95, and started jogging as soon as my smart watch buzzed at 2 km.

I knew what was going to happen. You probably know what was going to happen. Tim and Birger knew what was going to happen. Anybody who's done any reading on the subject knows what was going to happen.

Let me tell you, I was still surprised.

I ran to the end of the street, I ran up the road, I ran past my street, and I kept running non-stop, longer than I'd previously run in the weeks, actually, years, prior. I felt better running. I asked myself, "Do I like running?"

Probably not, but with this single test, I realized that your breathing can change how your entire body works. Kind of makes me question what else breathing could do for me moving forward and why I haven't been taught more about it growing up.

II. The Bargaining Phase

When I first found myself grappling with the intensity of a mid-life crisis, the whole idea seemed surreal. After all, how could someone like me, who had always prided themselves on mental fortitude and strength, suddenly feel so adrift? As I was confronted with my aging self, I felt an urgent need to reclaim my youth, if not at least feel like a younger version of myself.

That's when I found myself in the bargaining stage, seeking out ways to negotiate my way back into a sense of control. Two strategies became pillars of my journey – cold bathing and breathwork.

Cold bathing wasn't my first instinct. But I was attracted to its promise of improved health and enhanced immunity. The act was uncomfortable, even excruciating initially. But there was something about immersing myself in the biting cold water, challenging my physical boundaries, that became symbolic of my struggle. It represented my attempt to regain control over the inevitable aging process, an intense negotiation with time itself.

As I gradually overcame the initial shock and discomfort, I felt an undeniable rush of energy. It was as if each cold bath was a small victory, pushing back against the years that were trying to catch up with me. The physical discomfort paralleled the emotional struggle of my mid-life crisis, and each successful bath felt like a testament to my resilience. You would not believe what you're capable of after you have a win as big as getting in ice-cold water every morning. It's a game-changer.

Then there was breathwork, an entirely different beast. It was less about the physical challenge and more about the emotional and mental aspects. With every intentional inhalation and exhalation, I felt like I was clearing away the fog of confusion that had descended with the onset of my mid-life crisis. Breathwork became a way for me to negotiate with my inner turmoil and seek clarity amidst the storm.

It was as if my breath was the connection between my present and my past, helping me navigate through unresolved emotions and fears about the future. Through each breathing session, I felt more in tune with myself, gaining a more profound understanding of my desires, regrets, and aspirations. It was a means of self-discovery and emotional release, paving the way for self-growth in this complex stage of life.

My personal experiences with cold bathing and breathwork have taught me that bargaining in a mid-life crisis isn't just about seeking ways to delay or defy the aging process. It's about finding avenues to redefine your identity and regain a sense of control over your life.

While my journey with these practices continues, I also recognize the value of professional help. Having a therapist to guide me through these transitions would have most likely been invaluable. Although cold bathing and breathwork have been my strategies in dealing with this crisis, I encourage others going through a similar journey to find their unique paths, equipped with professional guidance and support. But again, you do you.

Remember, a mid-life crisis isn't merely a phase to endure or overcome. It's an opportunity for transformation and personal growth. Embrace the challenge and rise stronger.

III. The Pitfalls of Bargaining

When I found myself grappling with my mid-life crisis, I was surprised to see that my journey wasn't linear. Instead, it took me on a whirlwind ride through various stages, where each one unveiled a different piece of my fear, anxiety, and longing for the past. It was during the bargaining stage that I found myself flirting with danger.

In the thick of my crisis, I found solace in the cold. Cold bathing became my metaphorical life raft. It represented my attempt to regain control, negotiate with time, and reconnect with a vitality I thought I'd lost. The initial thrill was empowering, and I relished the thought of rediscovering my youthful resilience. But in retrospect, I see how my expectations were inflated.

I expected the cold baths to erase the years from my body, to transform me back into the person I was two decades ago. This unrealistic goal, to rewind time and return to my youth, burdened me with additional stress. I was fixating on the impossible while neglecting the very real opportunity to age with grace and mindfulness.

Don't get me wrong, at this point, I feel younger, stronger, faster, and all the things you'd feel reverse-aging, but there were points where I felt my mind disappearing into ways to quicken it all up. At one point, I was taking over 20 pills a day and NMN sublingually (aka under the tongue), to push the envelope. I searched the internet for the next thing I could ingest to make myself feel even better. It was exhausting.

My introduction to breathwork followed a similar pattern. I envisioned it as a miraculous fix-all that would alleviate my existential dread, all the while neglecting its inherent value as a tool for relaxation and self-awareness. I overburdened it with impossible expectations and thus turned a potentially beneficial practice into another source of stress.

My attempts to bargain with my age also began to seep into my personal relationships. I was in constant negotiation, not just with myself, but with my loved ones, craving their acceptance of my newfound routines and ways. I look back and realize the undue pressure I put on them, expecting them to understand and support my desperate attempts to reclaim my youth.

Through these personal experiences, I've learned that the bargaining stage of a mid-life crisis can be a slippery slope if we let it feed on our fears and insecurities. Unrealistic expectations can quickly turn beneficial practices like cold bathing and breathwork into sources of stress, rather than relief. Moreover, it can strain relationships as we engage in our personal tug-of-war with time.

What I wish to convey is that a mid-life crisis can be a chance for introspection and growth if we approach it with a balanced perspective. In our attempts to negotiate with time, we must not lose sight of the present and the reality of our circumstances. Bargaining should become a mindful transition towards acceptance and appreciation of our evolving selves, not a battle.

IV. The Illusion of Control

Control – a four-letter word with the power to incite fear and create illusions. In my twisted mid-life crisis circus, it was the lion I was desperately trying to tame. Who knew that the bargaining phase would transform me into an amateur lion tamer, complete with the hat and whip?

As I danced with the cold, immersed myself in breathwork, and demanded approval from my loved ones, I was essentially attempting to seize control. I imagined myself as the grand puppeteer, manipulating the strings of my life with an iron grip as if I could choreograph the tides of time to the beat of my own drum.

In my quest for control, I turned to cold bathing and breathwork. This was my grand plan – to reclaim my youth through sheer will and a series of shockingly cold plunges. The chill of the water was meant to wash away the looming shadow of age. Each breath I drew was supposed to infuse me with the power to go back in time. As if the mere act of puffing my chest like a proud pigeon and braving icy waters could magically roll back the years.

In reality, I was merely navigating through an illusion of control. The cold bathing and breathwork certainly had their benefits, but they were not the magic wands I had convinced myself they were. No amount of bargaining, no degree of cold or controlled breathing can stop the march of time or revert the changes it brings.

Perhaps the most hilariously tragic part of my misguided control escapade was my attempt to orchestrate the reactions and emotions of my loved ones. I wanted their acceptance, their admiration, and their validation. Little did I realize that I was trying to control something as unpredictable and chaotic as human emotions. I might as well have tried to control the weather.

The truth, as I've now come to realize, is that control, especially during a mid-life crisis, is often an illusion. We may convince ourselves that we're in the driver's seat, masterfully steering our lives. But in actuality, we're more like passengers in our aging family friend's car, clutching the safety bar, while praying to make it to our destination in one piece (this may just be me, but we've all been in that car).

Life, my friends, is not a puppet show, and we are not its puppeteers. Trying to assert control over time, our bodies, or others can lead to more stress and turmoil than the mid-life crisis itself. The sooner we accept that we cannot control everything, the better equipped we are to face the ride with a smile, a shrug, and maybe even a snarky comment or two. And perhaps that's the best way to navigate this mid-life circus after all.

V. Summary

In this chapter, I shared my experiences with breathwork and cold baths during my mid-life crisis, which I identified as part of my 'bargaining' phase. Feeling out of my element, I attended a breathwork masterclass, discovering the transformative potential of my own breathing, and even experienced a psychedelic-like state by merely breathing. This was a clear indication to me that breathing could fundamentally change how my body and mind functioned.

I also dabbled with cold baths, finding a sense of empowerment and control that I craved during this confusing period. These practices were my negotiation tactics, a bid to reclaim my past vitality and exercise control over my aging self. However, while they offered a sense of control and were tools for self-discovery, they were not a cure-all solution.

As empowering as these tactics were, there were certain pitfalls that I encountered during this bargaining phase. I developed unrealistic expectations from these practices, burdening myself with the stress of returning to my youth. My attempts to negotiate with time also began affecting my personal relationships as I sought acceptance of my new routines.

In retrospect, I see that I was lost in the illusion of control. I thought I could tame the inevitable progression of time through cold bathing and breathwork. I tried to puppeteer my life, only to realize I was navigating through an illusion of control. Bargaining with life shouldn't become a relentless pursuit of the past but rather a mindful transition towards accepting and appreciating our evolving selves.

As we move to the next chapter, "Depression," I invite you to join me as I continue to delve deeper into my mid-life journey. This phase brings its own set of unique challenges and discoveries. Depression is often viewed as a negative, but as we'll see, it can also provide opportunities for growth and self-discovery. In this period of seeming darkness, I found sparks of light that guided me toward acceptance and understanding of this complex life stage. Stay tuned as we navigate this together, learning that even in our lowest points, there is a potential for transformation.

Chapter 5: Depression

From New York to Nowhere

I. Introduction (The memoir part)

Well well well, you thought it'd all be smiles and ice cream, didn't you? Welp, sorry to be the bearer of bad news, but life sucks sometimes. For this one, I'm going to actually go back a few years because I think more people need to understand what depression actually looks like.

When I first moved to New York, I was a fish out of water trying to figure out what I wanted to do with my life. In Pennsylvania I'd been doing the same job for years, I had a general idea of what was going on, and I was happy. Then, I moved to New York and after only a month had a job working for a recruiting agency across the street from Grand Central Station. Yes, it was a pay cut, but I was making it work.

Then more good news! If you've seen my videos on social, there's a goat tattooed on my right arm, it's from a website I had called Mourning Goats. I interviewed big authors from around the world, from Nick Hornby to Cheryl Strayed and about 60 others. After interviewing one particular author, they asked me if I had any intentions of publishing the interviews in a book.

At the time, I had not. The author said that they had a press and could make it happen if I wanted to.

Book One: Chewing the Page: The Mourning Goats Interviews, was born. You can probably find some old copies on Amazon.

After we made that book happen, I threw out that I had a novel that I'd love to show him, a social media satire called Gripped. He asked me to submit the first 50 pages to the team and we'd go from there. After I did, they wanted the rest (which wouldn't have been a problem if it was written, at that point I had it mostly outlined, but nowhere near complete). I told them that I could get them the rest in a month, "after a final edit."

Every morning I woke up at some ungodly hour to take the train into the city and write at a coffee shop that rhymes with Car Trucks, for hours before work, and wrap up a book that had no ending.

Guess what I did in a month? Wrote something like 75 pages, finished the book, sold it to them, and started doing stage readings throughout Brooklyn and New York City. Anyone who saw me from the outside would have said, this guy is killing it. You know the saying, "If you can make it in New York City, you can make it anywhere…"

That's when I told my mom that I was more unhappy than I'd ever been. I was drinking to the point of blacking out every week and somehow continuing a relationship (that would eventually end in a fiery explosion, figuratively, not literally, I'm pretty sure she's okay…) holding down a job at a recruiting agency (doing something I'd never done before), and paying my bills in one of the most expensive cities in the world.

Here's the thing about depression that no one tells you. It doesn't have to look like depression. It can look like success. Read that again. Depression can look like success. Depression can look like throwing yourself into work. It can look like the funniest person in the room with everyone hanging on their every word. It can look like working out or running insane distances out of nowhere (I once did a half-marathon in the winter, in a storm, out of nowhere. This isn't to brag, it's to tell you that depression is weird). It can look like a lot of things, but the advice I can give on it is that it can also motivate you to make changes. You just have to choose to do something about it.

II. Depression and the Mid-Life Crisis

Depression is the life of a mid-life crisis party. The main squeeze. The big cheese. If a mid-life crisis were a pizza, then depression would be the anchovies - not everyone's favorite, definitely a bit salty, but for some, it adds a defining taste to the whole experience.

Depression often pops up uninvited during a mid-life crisis, much like that one work person who shows up to a happy hour with their funky hats and uncomfortable stares.

So why does a mid-life crisis bring depression along for the ride more often than not? You see, mid-life is a phase that likes to remind us of our mortality with the subtlety of a brick through the window. One day you're young, energetic, and full of dreams, and the next, you're staring at the white hair in your otherwise flawless red beard while grumbling about how loud the neighborhood kids are. It's a lot to take in. That grim reminder, that life's hourglass is continuously trickling sand, can leave us feeling a bit blue.

Speaking of feeling blue (or cold), let's talk about cold baths again, my companion through this whole rock show. Now, it may seem like an odd pairing, but ice bathing became my coping mechanism, my chilly meditation if you will. There's nothing like a sudden drop in body temperature to distract you from sad feelings.

But let's move away from metaphors and onto the science of this whole shebang. You see, depression is more than just feeling a little down. It's a real, tangible thing. It's caused by a complex interplay of genetic, biological, environmental, and psychological factors. And guess what can trigger it? Significant life changes and stress, like (surprise, surprise) a mid-life crisis.

When you're in your mid-life, your brain's dopamine levels start to dip (it's so easy to make a cold dip joke here, but I'll refrain). Dopamine, the feel-good neurotransmitter, takes a hit, and we start to feel less happy, less motivated, and less like our usual selves. It's a cruel joke of nature that just as we're grappling with the changes and challenges that mid-life brings, our brains decide to join the party too.

That depression also exacerbates everything above, especially denial (we'll talk about this more below). It takes your happiness, your motivation, and all of that, but denial? It strengthens. Making it even harder to see what's going on, let alone actually make the moves needed to get out of it.

Here's the plot twist. Despite the chill of the water and the depression, these cold baths became a source of enlightenment. As I submerged myself into the freezing abyss, I realized that sometimes, the best way to deal with life's cold realities is to confront them head-on. Ice baths were not just a physical challenge, they were a metaphorical embodiment of the discomfort that accompanies mid-life and depression.

Just like enduring the icy waters, enduring the mid-life crisis and depression isn't about resistance, it's about resilience. It's about understanding that this too shall pass. It's about hearing the voice inside your head, acknowledging it, and continuing forward.

So, every day, as I shivered in the cold water, I thought about all of this. I realized that feeling a little cold, a little uncomfortable, isn't such a bad thing. After all, no one said self-discovery would be a warm bubble bath. Sometimes, it's an ice bath on a frosty morning. And you know what? That's okay.

III. The Signs and Symptoms

Let's take a moment to step away from the icy, soul-searching soaks, and talk symptoms. The signs of depression are like pieces of a puzzle that you never signed up to complete. They're elusive, sneaky, and downright confusing. They show up unannounced, dressed in everyday clothing, and masquerade as routine aches and pains.

I told you I'd talk about denial again down here, it's time. As we slide through life's mid-life cry-sis. I was trying for a joke there, but let's move right along, shall we? As we move through our mid-life whatever, we have to pay attention to not only the way we feel but why we feel it. Denial will try and tell you that things are normal but are definitely not.

Take, for instance, the consistent fatigue that seems to drape over your every thought and action. It's not the "oh, I had such a long day" kind of fatigue. No, it's more the "I just ran a marathon while carrying a baby elephant on my back, and oh, I haven't slept in a week" sort of tired. The kind of tired where even my tired is tired, but... you haven't done anything that would cause that kind of tired.

And then there's the sleep. Oh, the irony. With such fatigue, you'd think I could sleep through a hurricane, right? Wrong. I would toss and turn, as though my bed was a raft lost at sea. The irony of it all, it would be laughable if it wasn't so frustrating. I would often retreat to my ice bath, seeking the cold's numbing touch to calm the restlessness. Many times I took second dips before bed to almost shock myself into sleep.

Remember joy? Neither did I. Once upon a time, I found pleasure in things. I delighted in the crunch of autumn leaves, the joy of biting into a perfectly ripe peach. But depression decided it was a party pooper and took away my invitation to the happiness hootenanny. Who says hootenanny? I really am in the mid-life, huh?

It's not all about emotions, though. Depression has a knack for making its presence felt physically. For me, it was back pain, as persistent and unwelcome as door-to-door salesmen. Recently, now that it has subsided a lot, I picture my depression like Sisyphus' rock, pushing the boulder up a hill over and over again, only to walk down get it again, and back to pushing. No matter what I did, that back pain would loop around and drop me.

One of the cruel ironies of depression is guilt. It's not enough that you're waging a war with your mind. One of the hardest demons I've fought is losing Kirsten AND depression knocking on my subconscious every day asking if I wanted to play. Having depression is one thing, but knowing that you have a good life, a steady job, and a loving family makes you question everything. I would often go to bed asking myself, "What right do I have to feel this way?"

Finally, I'd be remiss if I didn't mention the super fun and completely not horrible feeling of worthlessness. You start questioning your worth. The voice in your head, that cruel, critical narrator, comments on every flaw, every failure, every mistake you've ever made.

So, there you have it, my guide to the telltale signs of depression. A journey of persistent fatigue, disrupted sleep, loss of joy, relentless pain, guilt, and feelings of worthlessness.

IV. Tackling Depression: Strategies and Techniques

Welcome to the part of the book where we talk about strategies and techniques. This is where we dig into the toolbox, sharpen our pencils, and prepare to take the bull named Depression by its horns. Or, in my case, fill the tub with ice and grit your teeth.

First off, it's important to note that A. I'm not a doctor, just happen to have a bunch of letters after my name, and B. Dealing with depression is not a one-size-fits-all scenario. It's more of a tailored suit situation. What works for me might not work for you. It's a frustrating, labor-intensive process of trial and error that might make you want to scream into a pillow or punch the air. Trust me, I've been there, shivering in an ice bath, wondering what in the hell I was doing.

One of the first and arguably most crucial steps I would probably take today would be to talk to a professional. When I started my journey I felt pretty alone and wanted to figure it all out myself. I feel like it's that toxic vibe that many men have, where we can't reach out for help, we just have to figure it out ourselves. And I did. Either way, I think it would have been easier with some help.

But enough about professionals. Let's move on to the everyday stuff – the nitty-gritty of self-care. I've found that regular exercise – a jog around the block, a brisk walk in the park, or, dare I say it, a quick dip in an ice bath – can do wonders. The endorphins released during physical activity are nature's own brand of feel-good drugs. Regular exercise became as much a part of my recovery journey as ice bathing had become a part of my morning ritual (we'll get MUCH more into this in chapter 7).

Then there's mindfulness and breathwork, both of which were completely and totally out of my comfort zone when I started all of this. But trust me, there's something to it. Mindfulness is essentially being in the present, focusing on your body, your breath, and the sensations around you (grounding yourself…). It's about existing in the here and now, not ruminating on past failures or future worries. Another crucial aspect of tackling depression was my diet. I discovered that my depression didn't appreciate a steady intake of processed foods. Instead, it responded to a balanced diet rich in omega-3 fatty acids, lean proteins (so much protein), fruits, and vegetables. This was a learning curve, as my comfort food had to be replaced with healthier alternatives (again, you'll see in Chapter 7).

Lastly, never underestimate the power of a good night's sleep. I am positive that I'm not the only one, but for a long time, I'd go to bed at a respectable hour, no really, 9 or 10 o'clock. But, and it's a big but, I'd scroll on my phone or tablet until well past midnight, sometimes later, for absolutely no reason. I think one of the biggest changes in my overall health stemmed from more sleep. Try it for one week, no scrolling in bed, just sleeping, and see what happens. The worst thing it could do is cause you to miss a late-night Instagram update from your favorite celeb…

Tackling depression isn't a sprint; it's a marathon, a long and winding journey filled with self-care, mindfulness, healthy eating, and quality sleep. It's about finding what works for you, tweaking your strategies, and keeping at it. It's not easy, but I promise you, it's worth it.

V. Summary

In the chapter we just finished, we tackled the complex issue of understanding, recognizing, and dealing with depression during a mid-life crisis. I shared my personal experiences and the realization that depression can look like success, throwing myself into work, or even undertaking seemingly unrelated tasks with great intensity. Despite the outward appearance of success, internally I was wrestling with sadness, a relentless sense of fatigue, and a general loss of joy in activities that used to thrill me. These were my silent struggles, my invisible battle scars that no one else could see.

We talked about the intricacies of a mid-life crisis, how it often accompanies depression, and why. As we navigate through life, the stark reality of our mortality begins to set in. The stress of significant life changes combined with dipping dopamine levels in the brain can trigger depression.

We also discussed the various signs and symptoms of depression, from persistent fatigue and disrupted sleep to a loss of joy, guilt, and feelings of worthlessness.

Finally, we explored different strategies and techniques to combat depression, such as seeking professional help, regular exercise, mindfulness and breathwork, a balanced diet, and ensuring a good night's sleep. It's important to remember that what works for one person may not work for another, so it's crucial to find a tailor-made approach that suits you best.

In the next chapter, "The Upward Turn," we'll discuss how cold bathing might just be the biggest step to changing the rest of your life. For me, it changed my entire mindset, and we're not just talking about my constant need to talk about cold baths, it changed my entire mental state and I can't wait to share how it might do the same for you.

Chapter 6: The Upward Turn

Catching the Lifeline of Cold Baths

I. Introduction (The memoir part)

All right! Let's talk about the upward turn am I right? As I said above, I started cold bathing after I saw a bunch of videos on social media (most likely during one of those late-night scrolling sessions that we just talked about).

From the end of January through the beginning of February, my parents from Pennsylvania came to visit us here in Denmark. I told my dad I wanted to do it and he supported me (as he always does) in these weird decisions. He went with me to a bunch of hardware stores and outdoor stores looking for some kind of container that would hold enough water. I really wanted a 100-gallon Rubbermaid stock tank, but alas, couldn't find one and wanted to do it immediately. Eventually, we ended up at Bauhaus, a big home improvement store here in Denmark.

They had a few plastic pond liners that could have worked, but eventually, I ended up choosing a big rectangle-shaped pond basin that held about 100 gallons but was in no way made to be self-standing.

We got it home, put it down next to the solidly reinforced garage, and started filling it with water from the hose.
I was not going to waste any time.

With my dad filming and my mom, fiance, and son watching from the side in full winter outfits, I slammed my chubby (mostly naked) body in and felt a shock like I'd never experienced prior or since.

Between bouts of hyperventilation (which you can see in the video on social), I managed to stammer out, "I totally get it now! Oh yeah, it makes you breathe super weird. Oh wow… that was nutty!" My first icy rendezvous lasted a shivering 2:35 minutes. On day two, I braved the overnight-chilled water for a daring 3:10 minutes. Within 7 days, I had a 1000-liter intermediate bulk container (IBC) delivered and was ready for my first real DIY cold tub setup, not just a big black tub on the side of the garage.

The day after I received it, I pried open the top, filled it with water, and got into 4-degree water.

Something happened after that first dip. It changed me in ways that I can't really explain. And as I'm typing this out, I'm watching the videos from those first dips. On one side, I see the happiness that I had getting into the water, and on the other, I can see a deeply unhappy man, with too much weight on his bones, trying to push a big stone up a hill.

Looking at my face in those videos, I barely recognize the person staring back at the camera. In no way will I tell you all that ice bathing will transform you into a different person, because as I said previously, everyone is different, but for me, I will never be that guy again.

It's incredibly eye-opening to reflect on where I was, who I was, and what I was feeling in those first few dips. It's a special feeling seeing him through my new eyes. Even just a few months later, I'm a completely different person. And it's true, without ice bathing, I would have never been able to become the person I see in the mirror every day, because it's hard to look at someone every day who you don't respect.

This is about the upward turn though, so let's focus on who I've become, not where I've been.

II. Building Mental Fortitude With Cold Baths

We talked about a lot of the benefits of cold bathing in Chapter 3, but what I want to focus on next is the mindset that cold bathing creates. This is especially important before we jump into the Reconstruction chapter.

For me, there were 3 huge psychological benefits to getting in the water every day.

1. Embracing discomfort: As the saying goes, "What doesn't kill you makes you stronger" – or in this case, "What doesn't freeze you solid makes you more resilient." By willingly subjecting myself to the icy clutches of an ice bath, I've trained my mind to cope with discomfort. There's something to be said about someone who knows they are about to feel something horrible and still moves forward into that discomfort. There's a saying that goes something like, "Courage isn't the absence of fear, it's having fear but continuing anyway." while we're not going to

war, ice bathers know this feeling very well.

It's amazing what you can let slide off your back when you have this skillset built into your brain.

2. The power of ritual: We talked about ritual before, but in this case, it's about the calming effects of a daily routine. I've heard that a lot of people do something called a penguin plunge on New Year's Day, where they get into the nearest body of water in the dead of winter, once a year. I would guess that most of those people feel incredible when they leave the water, but alas, they only do it once a year. Imagine doing something every single day that blows your hair back and changes the trajectory of your entire day. That's ice bathing and that's the power of a ritual.

3. Achieving a Zen-like state: Definitely not the first time or the second, but after a handful of dips, something changes in your ability to handle the cold. As you slide into the frigid water, you can find yourself entering a state of profound inner peace. This is not to say that getting in is easy, because it never is, but it is something you can accept and embrace. As I tell my son, "You can do hard things," and so can Daddy.

III. Why Cold Baths Help in Reconstruction

I'll be touching on this in the next chapter too, but I think it deserves a section on the upward turn too, because it IS the upward turn I needed to get where I am today.

Starting on February 2nd, I got in water as cold as -3 Celsius every single day. There was not one day in February (or since, if we're being honest) that I wanted to get in that water, but I prevailed. That win is what we all need to be able to have the motivation to make a change.

No, you will not want to get in the water. No, you will not "enjoy" the water. No, most of your friends and family will not understand. But… at the end of a month, you start noticing that even though your body tells you not to get in the water, your mind is strong enough to tell your body to do it, and it listens.

Those wins you get, every single morning, are the treats you give your dog to teach it to sit and shake hands. Think of it this way; currently, when you wake up, you may have a coffee or a nice breakfast and then you're off to work. How do you feel (besides more awake, hopefully)?

Now, imagine a world where every morning you wake up and someone hands you a crisp $100 when you roll out of bed. You can feel it in your hand right now, can't you? Are your cheeks rising into a smile holding it? THAT is the win you need to make changes. THAT is cold bathing.

If you've never done a cold bath, I've compared the mental resilience that you gain from it to getting into a cold pool. You know that pause that most people have before jumping in? The one where they dip their toes in and talk about how cold it is, and how much they don't want to get in? With cold bathing, you learn to bypass that discussion and just do it. You understand that the benefit is worth the bad.

Being able to do this is insanely empowering and it bleeds over to a lot of other areas of your life. You're happier. You answer questions quicker, you speak easier, you say you're going to do something and then you do it because your mind has been trained to do so.

For all the people who ask, "Why do you get in cold water every day?"

This is the answer. My body and mind are comfortable with each other and my body does what my mind decides, not the other way around.

And now that you understand WHY we do what we do, it's time to do it yourself.

IV. Taking the Plunge: How to Get Started

Welcome, aspiring masochists, to the ultimate guide for constructing your very own sub-zero sanctuary. Say goodbye to the warm, comforting embrace of a hot shower, and hello to the bone-chilling thrill of a do-it-yourself ice bath. In this chapter, we'll walk you through the "thrilling" process of creating your personal torture chamber, complete with tips for selecting the perfect ice, achieving the ideal water temperature, and determining the optimal duration for your icy escapades. So, strap on your mittens and let's get started!

First Off: One Ice Bath Does Not Fit All...

As of today, I've been in 7 styles of ice baths. A weird plastic tub thing. A 1000-liter IBC water tank. One of the inflatable versions, that if you're already into cold bathing, have seen repeatedly across social media. One of the DIY chest freezer versions, that if you're into cold bathing, have seen repeatedly across social media. A fjord. A lake. And the ocean.

Let's quickly talk about the positives and negatives of each.

Man-made Ice Baths

Weird Plastic Tub:
Positives:
- Mine was $75
- Quick & Easy
- Readily available

Negatives:
- Mine had sharp edges
- Uncomfortable
- Too shallow
- No drainage

1000 Liter Water Tank:
Positives:
- It's huge
- So much room for activities
- In the winter, it's perfect…

Negatives:
- It's huge
- Lots to clean
- Hard to keep cold outside of winter
- Ice? You would need hundreds of pounds

Inflatable:
Positives:
- Cheap $50-$125
- Easy to clean
- Small footprint
- Portable

Negatives:
- Can pop
- Need a LOT of ice to keep cool in warmer temps
- May be too small for some

Chest Freezer (For a more in-depth article on how to make your own chest freezer cold bath, head to the blog on coldfeat.com):
Positives:
- Cold water, every day, no matter the outside temp
- No ice needed
- Fun to decorate
- More like D.I.Y(eahhhh)
- One size fits most (I recommend 350+ liters)

Negatives:
- A lot of work to build
- Maintenance
- If the fridge dies, it's just a big plastic tank
- Price $250+

Natural Ice Baths

As these are all natural bodies of water, I'll just list the specific features that are positive and negative here. The obvious positive for all of them is, cold bathing in nature is awesome, and for me, it always feels way more badass when you see people in coats as you take your clothes off to get in cold water. Negatives, it's more dangerous, you're not at home if you want to warm up quickly, only available in the colder months, weather, sharks…

Fjord:
Positives:
- Saying fjord is super fun

Negatives:
- Possibly sharks
- Stones?

Lake:
Positives:
- When they freeze you look at least 100x cooler getting in…

Negatives:
- Not sharks…
- Also stones?

Ocean:
Positives:
- There's something incredible about getting into the ocean in the winter with no wetsuit. You've been to the beach… now get in

Negatives:
- Sharks
- Being eaten by sharks
- Undertow
- I think that's it…

The EXTREMELY simplified instructions on how to start ice bathing? Here you go:

1. Select your vessel: Whether you prefer the claustrophobic confines of a plastic tub or the more difficult DIY route, the choice is yours. Just make sure it's watertight – because nothing ruins a good ice bath like a leaky container.

2. Fill 'er up: If you're in nature, skip this one… Once you've chosen your vessel, it's time to fill it with water. Usually, the water coming out of your hose is around 15 degrees Celsius, so it's a really good temperature to get you started.

3. Ice, ice, baby: If you're ready to make it colder, you're gonna need the pièce de résistance: ice. When it comes to ice, there's no such thing as too much. No, for real. Many people think that a bag or two will chill your water to where it needs to be, but it just won't cut it, especially in the summer.

4. Take the plunge: With your ice bath prepped and ready, it's time to dive in – figuratively speaking, of course. Submerge yourself slowly and cautiously, lest you shock your system into a state of permanent paralysis. Remember to breathe long, deep, and slow. Your body will want to hyperventilate, breathe through it. You can do this. And, especially the first time, do not push it too hard. Just test the waters. See how your body reacts.

Tips for Choosing the Perfect Ice, Water Temperature, and Duration

Now that you're well-versed in the art of ice bath builds, let's go into the finer details of crafting the ultimate ice bath experience:

1. The ice: Test for yourself, but you're going to most likely need 20+ bags of ice to get it where it needs to be. When it comes to ice, I've found that bigger is better and if you get a food delivery service, they'll often offer up free re-freezeable ice bags that do wonders.

2. The water temperature: While the ideal ice bath temperature varies depending on your level of masochism (I keep mine around 3), most dippers recommend a range between 0-15°C (32-59°F). Any colder, and you risk frostbite; any warmer, and you'll miss out on the full "pleasures" of the ice bath

experience.

3. The duration: How long should you subject yourself to the icy embrace of an ice bath? The answer is simple: as long as you want. Most mortals aim for 1-5 minutes but feel free to adjust as necessary based on your personal pain tolerance. Dr. Susanna Søberg says that you only need around 11 minutes a week, so feel free to test what works for you and do that.

And there you have it: a tongue-in-cheek guide to crafting your very own DIY ice bath. With a little practice and a lot of patience, you'll soon be well on your way to becoming a bona fide ice bath connoisseur.

V. Maintaining the Habit

Okay, now that you've seen everything above, you might be itching to hop into the nearest body of cold water. But let me tell you - the cold is a cruel mistress. It can bite, and it will test your will. Doing it every day is almost impossible. However, I'm here to share some tips and motivation to help you stick to the habit.

1. Remember the 'why': Whenever you're inching towards that tub, remember why you started. Remember the benefits you're seeking, whether it's improved circulation, boosted mood, or better sleep. Visualize that end goal. If you're anything like me, you might even start to see the ice water as the reason behind your entire transformation.

2. Baby steps: Even though I didn't listen to this tip, diving headfirst into an ice bath on day one is a surefire way to make sure there's no day two. Start small. A cold shower for a few minutes a day, gradually increasing the time as your

body adjusts. Before you know it, you'll be soaking in an ice bath like it's a hot tub.

3. Embrace the shock: Let's face it - the cold is shocking, but that's the beauty of it. Every gasp is a reminder that you're alive and kicking. Each dip is a miniature battle against your comfort zone. With each victory, you're not just a bit more immune to the cold, but also a bit more resilient in life.

4. Accountability: It's easy to hit the snooze button on a solo alarm, but when you've got a partner in frost, it's a different game. Find a fellow cold bather or consider posting your journey online. The simple act of recording where you've come from is a magical thing once you've been in it for a few months. My first videos are a completely different person than I am now, it's insanely humbling.

5. Celebrate your victories: Every minute you spend in that icy embrace is a triumph. So, don't be shy about celebrating. Do a victory dance, treat yourself to a hot cocoa, or post a victorious ice-bathing selfie with the red glow we've all learned to love. For my 100th dip, I jumped in 10 different natural ice baths. For my 200th, I'll release this book. ;-)

6. Laugh at yourself: Yes, you might look like a frozen turkey on Thanksgiving in there. And yes, your yelps might be a bit high-pitched. But hey, where's the fun if you can't laugh at yourself? Let your ice bath be a reminder to not take life too seriously. This is a necessity for me, especially on my social channels. Some days were hard, really hard, humor helps ease the pain.

7. Reflect: Every day you get in is a win, don't forget to reflect on all the incredible things you're doing in the water and out. As the all-knowing Ferris Bueller once said, "Life moves pretty fast. If you don't stop and look around once in a while, you could miss it."

The last thing I'll say on this is about how little your time in the water actually is. If you break it down, it's 1-5 minutes out of 1440 minutes in your day. Think about that. In the grand scheme of life, an ice bath is a drop in the ocean. But it's a drop that can ripple into transformation. So next time the cold beckons, take a deep breath, take the plunge, and remember - the ice might be cold, but the glow of self-improvement is warm enough to keep you going. Embrace the chill.

VI. Summary

There you have it! We dove headfirst into the icy depths of cold bathing. If I remember correctly, we started this frosty adventure on the back of some late-night social media spirals and wound up standing in a garden pond liner. The lengths we'll go to for a mid-life crisis, am I right?

But beyond the frostbite and hyperventilation, we dipped our toes into some serious science too. Between cold shock proteins being released like confetti at a parade and our mammalian diving reflex working overtime, who would have thought an icy dunk could do so much? From better sleep to less stress and even an elevated mood, it's like having your very own wellness retreat in your backyard. A very very cold wellness retreat.

The shocking part wasn't the cold water - although, let's be honest, that first dunk was like hugging a polar bear. No, it was how this simple routine had such a profound impact on how I saw my past, present, and future. I used to see a guy pushing a big rock uphill, and now? I see a mountain climber ready for the next peak.

Now that we're all seasoned Polar Bears, it's time to move on to the next chapter, aptly named "Reconstruction" (puts on a hard hat and pulls out blueprints).

We're going from the North Pole to the gym and the grocery store, focusing on health, diet, weight loss, and strength training. But don't worry, there'll be less frostbite and more delicious, nutritious foods and a dash of 'feel the burn.' "Reconstruction" is all about building a stronger, healthier, and happier you during this mid-life whirlwind. We'll dive into the nitty-gritty of a balanced diet (brace yourself, protein is coming, so much protein), strength training (picture Popeye after his spinach), and the ins and outs of weight loss (adios, love handles).

Ready to reconstruct your life one ice cube, one push-up, and one plate of veggies at a time? Then, bring on the broccoli, the barbells, and of course, the bathing suits!

Chapter 7: Reconstruction

Building the New You

I. Introduction (The memoir part)

So now that we're here, how can you actually use any of this to help you? Well, for me, every weight loss journey I've been on has ended in sadness. It ended with the short-lived weight I lost coming back stronger than ever. But now, with cold bathing, breathwork, and a solid focus on my physical health (including not eating like an idiot), I've built a foundation, a regimen, an easy-to-follow base, that anyone can use. Like I said in the first line of the book, "I am not special." You can do this.

That being said, you have to make it through two months to even get to the losing weight stage of this. In every other weight loss program on the planet, they expect you to dive right in, don't eat carbs, don't eat cookies, don't eat an entire family-sized pizza three meals a day... it's almost impossible to do this because we straight-up don't have the willpower to do so.

I remember during the breathwork lessons with Tim how he spoke about making sure that especially when you start, that you don't take on too much, because if you do, you won't come back to it the next day.

This is kinda like that.

II. The 6-Step Plan for Fixing You

Step One - Hate Yourself

This may sound odd, but this isn't a weight loss method for someone already in shape. Step One is to hate yourself. I know, I know, "but Jason, that doesn't sound healthy." You're right, and neither was I. As I write this, I'm still a work in progress, but I'm getting there. Step One is all about looking in the mirror and hating waking up to see that every day.

For some people, myself included, my transition to unhealthy took years. I didn't see it happening until that faithful day at the Hillerød Kommune I mentioned earlier. But when I did, I couldn't not see it every time I saw my reflection. I couldn't not see it every time I took my shirt off. I grimace every time I felt a roll of skin fold over on itself. Too much? Okay, moving on.

Unless you hate the version of yourself you've become, the rest is going to be much harder.

Step Two - Month One - This Water is Like... Cold Cold

Congratulations, you've made it to step two... or, I'm sorry, it's hard to hate yourself. I was there. I feel you.

This is the first month of two that will start you on your journey. This is also where we start ice bathing. Before we begin, let me tell you why we do it. Some of this I went over in the last chapter, but hear me out.

This step is not necessarily about ice bathing, it could be about the sauna or walking or cold showers or whatever, but the thing you choose, has to be horrible AND something you're willing to do every day for an entire month (if I was you, I'd make it cold bathing, because that's what this book is about, right?). February is a shorter month, it's when I started, so you're welcome to game the system and do the same.

Month one isn't about losing weight. That's gotta feel good to hear. You've decided to lose weight and for an entire month, you don't have to worry about it. There are other things to worry about, don't you worry, but weight isn't one of them and it can't be, yet.

Month one is about learning that you're capable of losing weight. Every other weight loss program I've heard about says that you have to go from 0 - 100 on day one. You no longer eat carbs, you only eat vegetables, you only eat butter, you only cheat on even days, I don't know... whatever they say. This program knows that unfortunately, you don't hate yourself (step one) without giving up your willpower, especially toward eating.

This goes back to Tim's breathing techniques, if it's too hard, you won't do it. I know you. You know you. We get it.

Step two forces willpower into your brain. Step two shows you that every single day, you can wake up and do something hard to start your day and you can be alright. I said this before and in one of my videos, but, there are 1,440 minutes a day, you can give 1-5 to ice water.

For the first week, it will be hard.
For the second week, it will also be hard.
Week three, it'll be easy. Just kidding, it will also be hard.
Finally, week four, it's gonna be hard then too.

Cold bathing isn't easy, it's something that you get more and more used to doing, but it never gets easier.

The best part of ice bathing first thing every day, is that you challenge yourself every morning and you win every morning, before most people around the world have started their routine, you're already one win in. It's an incredible feeling to know that after that five minutes (or however long you decide to stay in) no matter what you do next, you already beat that day. You won and no one can take that away.

After a month of winning, it's time for step three.

Before we get there, take a deep breath in, it's going to be a hell of a transition.

Step Three - Month 2 - Are You Mad? OMAD… One Meal a Day

To answer your question, yes. I am mad. Crazy. Insane. Whatever you want to call me, but for me, this is the only thing that made me strong enough to do what I knew I needed to do.

I could not have done step three without doing step two. Step two gave me the willpower to actually follow through with what needed to happen next.

Step three is one meal a day for one month (I suggest dinner so that you can keep a solid schedule with family and friends. If you think about it, the first two meals of the day are more often than not, solo).

Hear me out.

However, you got to the place you are. You weren't thinking about what you were eating. You were throwing sugar and snacks and carbs and proudly downing eight tacos for dinner, telling yourself that you could probably keep eating tacos after dinner and into your nightly TV binge.

Doing one meal a day is hard. You're fasting for twenty-three hours and eating for one. It's really hard.

There is a benefit, to that one meal, eat whatever you want. Eat the 8 tacos, eat the pizza, eat the steak and potatoes, eat whatever you crave, but start thinking about where you'll go after the month is over.

The reason we're doing this step is because your food choices have been shite up until now. You wouldn't hate yourself if they were good choices, right? Step three brings food choices (or lack thereof) to your regimen. Step three takes the willpower you learned from step two and forces you to completely and totally change your food consumption routine. And trust me, you'll need this in step four.

For many of us, our day is simply separated by food breaks. Think about it. Wake up, eat, go to work, snack, work, lunch, work, snack, commute, dinner, rest, snack, sleep, repeat. It's do the thing, feed, do the thing, feed, all day, every day. OMAD forces you to disrupt the way you do things. It forces you to reconsider the way you eat and the necessity for constant food breaks.

Don't get me wrong, I love food, I love food breaks, but, and it was a big butt, my food breaks were full of bad choices that I didn't truly understand until I reconfigured my way of getting nutrition.

After one month of OMAD, your food clock is reset. Most likely, you're noticing that you don't need food all the time. You ravage the food you do eat in that hour, but you're pounding water/black coffee/tea all day and aren't hungry all the time. This means it's time for step four.

Step Four - Month Three - The "Diet" and Exercise Part

If you've completed the first two months, you are already WELL on your way to making this happen. Congratulations!

Here's where we start the real work. Like I said at the beginning. I wanted, nay, needed to lose over 60 pounds. Step four is where the real work sets in. Now is the time when you start the diet and the exercise. Hopefully, the first three steps have put a voice in the back of your head leading up to this part that says, I need to work, I need to burn this new energy, I want to move around.

The Diet

You can use my method, which is completely self-made and probably insane, or any other weight loss diet you think makes sense to you. But know, that the first few steps above were done to give you the power to make the diet feasible. Having the big win in the morning from cold bathing gives you the willpower, having the one meal a day gives you the feeling like any meals that you have moving forward are cheat meals. It's all about reworking your brain.

Before we get to my diet, I want you to hear me say this one more time, feel free to use any diet out there that you think makes sense for you. Those first two months give you the power to do it. You just have to do it.

Jason's Extreme Diet

First off, I guessed that I wouldn't be taking in all the necessary vitamins that I needed through what I planned to eat, so I loaded up on a whole bunch of supplements. They looked like this.

Morning Supplements:
- NMN
- Caffeine
- Fish Oil
- Lion's Mane
- MACA

Afternoon Supplements:
- Biotin
- Tumeric

- Marine Collagen

Evening Supplements:
- Multivitamin
- Vitamin D
- Fish Oil
- MACA

As I said above, my diet was all about protein and keeping myself constantly satiated. The biggest issue I had before doing things the way I've laid out here was being hungry and eventually just quitting whatever the diet was because I couldn't stand being hungry. This time, I wasn't going to let that be a thing. Below is an average day and honestly, most days looked a lot like this for a solid six months.

Morning:
- Burger-sized ground beef
  - Cayenne pepper
  - Salt
  - Rosemary
- Overeasy Egg

Snack:
- Protein Bar (20g protein)

Afternoon:
- Chicken or Beef Jerky
- Protein Chips (I found mine on Amazon)
- Protein Bar (20g protein)

Evening
- A small portion of dinner (most likely a "normal portion" for healthy people, but always seemed small to me).
- Wasabi Nori (20 calorie box)

Before we move to the exercise I need you to read this next part and actually take it into account for your program. I LOVE burgers. I LOVE eggs. I LOVE chicken and beef jerky.

This diet wasn't hard for me because of this. Make sure that your diet is something you can follow. Make it so yummy for YOU, that you can't fail. Just make sure that the things you pick are solid in protein and low in carbs. There are a million protein bars on the market. The protein bars I ate are by far the best-tasting bars on the planet, they're called Barebells Protein Bars and I love all the flavors. They are awesome for me and taste great. Find your own.

Oh, and that final snack of seaweed is more about telling my inner snacky-boi to shut it, they're 20 calories and perfect to do this. For the entire time, I didn't eat anything after 7 pm, every night, meaning for at least 12 hours a day, I was fasting. Always remember that sleeping is a great time to rack up your fasting time.

Speaking of Fasting

I'd be remiss if I didn't mention this. Three months in, I saw my weight loss plateau a bit, so I started doing 48-hour fasts every two weeks. I'm not going to pretend I know all the benefits of them, but please look into it for yourself. It did wonders for helping me push through. It also helped me with mental clarity while putting this book together. It's incredible what the body is capable of when you push it more than it's ever been pushed.

The Exercise

Do whatever you want for exercise. Do what you're comfortable with. But, for me, I had 3 tricks to lose the weight and I really hope that number 3 will change your life too.

1. Day in and day out, no matter what, I would hit 10,000 steps. Every day. Without fail. For my son's routine, we take a shower before he goes to bed. If I finish, put him down, and my watch says 8,292… I'm going to go for a walk. It's funny how fast you figure out how many steps things are in your neighborhood. "Oh, I need 2,000 steps, I'm going to walk/jog around the big loop." "600 steps, gotta circle the block." And so on.

2. I think if you're reading this book, you're aware of Dr. Andrew Huberman. If not, go check him out, he's incredible. In one episode he says, "In the morning, get up, and either run or get on some exercise bike and just pedal like someone's chasing you with a syringe full of poison." Not only does this help hit your 10k a day, but it also dives into your body fat stores quicker, because you don't have any food/carbs to grab energy from. Most days you can catch me outside rowing and then jogging before cold bathing.

3. Hi, this is a big one that not enough people consider. Instead of snacking on chips, snack on working out. I know it sounds ridiculous, but again, it worked for me. Throughout this whole journey, I worked from home. At one point in it, I put a pull-up bar right outside my office door. Every time I walk in, I do a pull-up, every time I walk out, I do a pull-up. It's NOTHING… but those pull-ups add up. Next to my desk, I have kettlebells, I have parallette bars, push-ups, dips, and simple bar hangs, and do them throughout the day. This isn't a workout, it's just a taste of a workout, but for me, I went from hardly being able to do A SINGLE PULL-UP (which I'm still in denial about) to easily doing 10… Actually, I'm

going to go do 10 and then continue writing. You wouldn't believe how fast you change your max number if you're consistent.

I didn't know where I was going to put this anecdote, but here we are. Do you know what happens around the four-month mark that's scary? For me, it was scary to start doing something for my workout or stretching or whatever, because my willpower, my drive, or whatever you want to call it, was so strong, that I knew, if I started something, I would continue doing it for the long term. I didn't want to start a stretching routine every morning because I would do it EVERY morning. I didn't want to make my routine too difficult, or too hard, or too… whatever… not because I couldn't do it, but because I WOULD do it.

Whatever your exercise plan is, make sure that it's hard enough to burn calories, but easy enough to do without fail. If you're not reaching the goal every day or most days, it's too hard, and if you fail enough, you'll feel shitty and will begin to not do it at all.

Trust me on this one. I hated myself for a reason. I let myself accept excuses every single day for eating shitty, drinking shitty, not working out, and feeling like absolute dogshit every day for far too long.

Give yourself a plan that lets you do it for the long term, not just next week.

Read that again.

Step Five

Do the stuff above until you're healthy. Whatever that looks like to you. This could be a specific weight (within reason), it could be a size (within reason), or it could be a "look" (within reason).

Don't allow yourself to lose. You already won first thing in the morning. Keep winning for the entire day and the rest of your life.

And if you cheat or eat shitty at some point, don't lose your mind, just get back on the horse, it's all about the journey, not just the race to get there.

Step Six

Moving forward, test new things in one-month increments.

No one wants to live in a crazy calorie deficit forever. But (and this is a smaller butt) be careful about diving back into your "regular" diet. We're still the same person we were in step one, hopefully, a healthier version, but we can easily slip into bad habits. Be careful about going crazy into eating "whatever you want" right out of the gates. It's time for a healthy lifestyle, not just getting healthy and going back to step one.

You got this.

III. Summary

My former self was a chubby guy fond of pizzas, tacos, and everything unhealthy. So, one day, I looked in the mirror and loathed what I saw. But that self-loathing sparked a life-changing journey, one that started with cold baths. But after a month of freezing my skin off, I found that I could survive. It was my first win, a 'cold' realization of my willpower.

The second step? One Meal A Day (OMAD). Sounds mad, right? But it's not about starvation; it's about realizing that you don't need to constantly feed yourself to survive. And guess what? You get to stuff your face with whatever you want for that one meal.

Third, dieting and exercise. My 'extreme' diet was more protein and less carbs. And the exercise? 10,000 steps a day, no excuses, even if I had to roam around the block at night.

So there you have it - the not-so-secret recipe of my transformation: icy self-reflection, mad eating habits, a protein-packed diet, 10,000 steps, and bite-sized workouts from pull-ups to kettlebell swings. They worked for me and I'm pretty sure they'll work for you.

But remember, the first step is always the hardest, and in this case, the second is freezing your ass off.

Chapter 8: Working Through

The Art of Pushing Onward

I. Introduction (The memoir part)

Now that we've talked about the weight loss and health side of things, you have to wonder, "Can I do this? Or, am I capable of this?" First off, stop it. We're not going to continue living in this weird question of if we can, we're just going to do.

The following story will make sense once we get to the end, but trust the journey. One morning I woke up deciding that I wanted a bigger win than just the daily cold bath. Up until this particular day, my fastest 5k run in the previous *cough* ten years, was around 35 minutes. Something made me want to destroy that time. And instead of thinking about it like I'd looked at many things in the past and questioning myself, much like the fictional version of you above, I just said, you're going to do this. You're going to take 6 minutes off your time and run a 5k in under 30 minutes.

I told Anna that I was going to do it, she, being the supportive partner she is, said, "You got this."

I wasn't going to row beforehand, I was just going to do it. I sat down on the couch, programmed in my Runkeeper app to whisper into my ear how far I'd run, how fast I'd run, and my pace, every .5 km. I tied the laces on my bright orange Asics, and put on some AGGRESSIVE music in my ears. We're talking Pantera, Disturbed, Product of Hate, and more… also, the opening of Thunderstruck may be the most motivational opening to any song ever in my eyes. Argue with me on that.

Anyway, when I started running, there was an app malfunction and she kept telling me at weird intervals what was going on, but after a minute or two, she figured it out and I fell into a solid groove.

Around the halfway point, I walked for a few steps to get some really deep breathing in. And then back to it. I actually walked 3-4 times but balanced those walks with a hard push forward.

The more I wanted to quit, the more I turned up the music, both volume and aggression. My times for each kilometer were:

1. 5:17
2. 6:15
3. 5:46
4. 5:56
5. 5:58

With a total time of 29:14! It's definitely not the fastest time in the world, but that's not the point of what I'm saying here. It's that, if you're a runner or getting into running, taking 6 minutes off your time in any way is incredible, but doing it only after a few weeks with pure mental fortitude? That's something to be proud of. That's a big win.

So all of this being said, I want you to consider that when you're working through your own battles, to believe in yourself. Another saying that I think we're all familiar with is, "If you think you can, or you think you can't, you're right." In this case, I set myself up with 10 reminders to speed up to make time, and I smashed my goal, just like I wanted. If you tell yourself you can, you're that much closer to actually doing it. You are what you believe.

You can do this shit. You just have to do this shit.

II. Understanding the Process

Hold on to your swimming trunks, because we're about to take a deep dive into the throbbing heart of darkness that is the mid-life crisis. Like, deep deep, Mariana Trench level. You may be asking yourself, "Why should I be bothering with this at all?" Well, the answer is as simple as this: working through a mid-life crisis is just as much a part of living as breathing, eating, and indulging in an occasional weekend Netflix binge.

Picture your mid-life crisis as a big, gnarly knot. Like the kind of knot you'd find in your favorite wired headphones after your two-year-old found them, conveniently in a case, on your desk, out of their reach, but somehow reached, opened, and then practiced their fine motor skills with. You don't just yank at it and hope it comes undone - that's a one-way ticket to Frustration City. No, you sit down, take a deep breath, and pick it apart bit by bit. It's the same with a mid-life crisis. Rushing through it is akin to pulling the string and hoping for the best. But, if you take the time to unravel the knot, you're more likely to find the solution and learn something about yourself along the way. Possibly about where you need to keep your headphones, but a lesson nonetheless.

Now, let's talk about why fast-tracking your mid-life crisis can lead to more harm than good. Think about it - when has rushing through anything complex ever led to a positive outcome? It's like trying to assemble IKEA furniture without looking at the manual or eating a bowl of hot soup in one gulp. In both cases, you're likely to end up with a wonky bookshelf or a burnt tongue, neither of which is a pleasant experience.

If you try to sprint through your mid-life crisis, you may miss out on the process of self-discovery and self-improvement. Yes, this introspection comes packaged with some uncomfortable feelings. But no one ever said the journey to self-realization would be a walk in the park (if they did, they're liars, and you should probably stop listening to them).

A mid-life crisis is an opportunity to look inward and take stock of your life. It's a time to reflect on where you've been, where you are, and where you want to go. It's a time to confront the big, scary questions like, "What is my purpose?" or "Why do I need to get in ice water to actually make progress?" That last one hit home. I assume picking up this book at all will be a question for many of you at this point. Anywho, rushing through these important introspective periods is like skipping leg day at the gym. Do these guys not understand how silly they look? Reminds me of the movie, So, I Married an Axe Murderer when Mike Myers says, "It's like an orange on a toothpick."

So, resist the urge to rush. Give yourself the space to feel all those weird, wonderful, and woeful emotions. Let your mid-life crisis be the existential car wash it needs to be, scrubbing off the grime of doubt and confusion to reveal the shiny, hopefully-not-rusty, chassis of your being underneath. Reflect.

III. Coping Strategies

Over the years I've accumulated a few coping mechanisms, but let's get one thing straight. Coping mechanisms are like cold tubs - one size does not fit all. You have to try on a few to find out what fits and what just doesn't do it. So, keep an open mind and a flexible spirit as we delve into the world of mindfulness, self-compassion, and stress management.

First on the docket: Mindfulness. Now, I know it sounds a tad fancy, like something you'd find on the menu at an upscale fusion restaurant, but trust me, it's simpler than you think. Essentially, mindfulness is about being present in the moment. It's about acknowledging your thoughts, emotions, and sensations without judgment.

During my mid-life crisis, I found that grounding and breathwork for a few minutes each day had a remarkably calming effect. Kind of like watching clouds float by in the sky, except the clouds are your thoughts, and the sky is, well, your mind. Also… the clouds in Denmark are out of this world, so feel free to literally just watch the clouds, wherever you are.

Next up, we've got self-compassion. This one's a biggie. When navigating a mid-life crisis, you'll likely run into the nasty little gremlin called self-doubt. He's not a pleasant chap, always whispering mean things about failures and unmet goals. I found it incredibly helpful to counteract his spiteful whispers with some good ol' self-compassion. Basically, treat yourself like you would treat a dear friend - with kindness, understanding, and a hefty dose of love. For me, self-compassion involved speaking kindly to myself, even when I messed up or felt lost. And as weird as it might be, reminding myself that I am only human (especially on the days my scale went UP when I was working so hard.

Finally, we've got stress management. This is the Swiss Army knife of coping strategies. It has a tool for every occasion, whether it be regular physical exercise, a balanced diet, or even just a simple, cathartic, scream-into- your-pillow moment. My personal favorite, though, is humor. Yeah, I know - who'd have thought? For me, laughing at my circumstances, no matter how grim, lightened the load and made everything feel a little less intimidating. Just be careful, there's a very thin line between lightening your load and destroying your well-being by constantly making yourself a joke.

And believe me, I know, these strategies might sound great on paper (or on your screen), but remember, it's not enough to know them. You've got to live them, practice them, like learning a new dance or trying to pronounce Worcestershire. It takes time, patience, and a good deal of trial and error. But, with persistence, they can become second nature.

Throughout my mid-life crisis, these strategies were as crucial as oxygen. They allowed me to navigate the murky waters with resilience and humor, even when the waves were a little choppy. So, take a leaf out of my book (literally and figuratively), and give these tools a whirl. Who knows, you might just find the right shoe that fits. And remember, at the end of the day, it's not about getting through a mid-life crisis unscathed; it's about growing through it, one mindful, compassionate, and stress-managed step at a time.

IV. Riding the Waves

Emotional waves are the uninvited guests of mid-life. They arrive abruptly, like a violent storm in the once-serene sea of our lives. These waves can be merciless, intimidating, and relentless. But trust me when I say, they can also be the catalyst to profound self-transformation.

There's a chilling beauty to these waves, a raw intensity that forces us to confront our deepest fears and insecurities. They bring us face-to-face with the relentless passage of time, the subtle changes in our reflection in the mirror, the dreams we haven't fulfilled, and the paths we didn't tread.

First, let's talk about the icy embrace of cold bathing. It sounds brutally uncomfortable, and believe me, it is. Like I talked about before, the first time the cold water wrapped itself around me, it was a physical shock that mirrored the emotional shockwave of my mid-life crisis. Yet, there was an inexplicable purity in that moment of absolute discomfort. As I resisted the numbing cold, I was, in a sense, building a resistance against the emotional waves threatening to engulf me. It was a testament to my resilience, my ability to withstand the storm.

Breathwork was my sanctuary. There's a reason I wear the bracelet that says, "Breathe." It was the tether that kept me connected to myself when the emotional waves threatened to carry me adrift. The rhythmic flow of air in and out of my lungs acted as a gentle reminder that I was still alive, still fighting, still here amidst the chaos. It grounded me, gave me a sense of control, and allowed me to ride the wave rather than being drowned by it.

The notion of physical transformation during mid-life is a bitter pill to swallow. It's a process that's often marked by self-doubt and frustration. I, too, struggled with the mirror's truth, but then I made a choice - to evolve with grace. I embraced my body, as it was, and I took on the challenge of refining it. I exercised, not just to mold my muscles but to build a shield of confidence and strength that no emotional wave could shatter.

And then came the art of working through it. I want to be extremely clear here, there's no sidestepping these emotional waves. No shortcuts, no detours. We must confront them head-on. It's a grueling journey, one that feels like an eternal struggle against a merciless current. But with every struggle, I learned something about myself, about my strengths, my weaknesses, and my capacity to endure. And this journey is never over, it's ongoing, and I'm taking steps every day to be better.

So here's my heartfelt advice to you: when the emotional waves of mid-life come crashing, embrace them. Let them soak you, let them overwhelm you, and then let them recede. Equip yourself with the tools of resilience - cold bathing, breathwork, physical transformation, and most importantly, the willingness to work through it all.

Always remember that the storm doesn't last forever and the waves do subside. And when they do, you'll find yourself standing taller, stronger, and more resilient than ever before. You are not just surviving the storm; you are thriving in it.

V. Summary

The first part of this journey involved a pivotal moment when I decided to smash my previous record of a 35-minute 5k run. Instead of doubting myself, as I had done so often in the past, I just declared, "I'm going to do this. I'm going to run a 5k in under 30 minutes." With some aggressive music and my Runkeeper app, I did it. I managed to run the 5k in 29:14, proving to myself that with determination, even daunting goals are achievable. I share this story not to brag about my running time, but to emphasize the power of self-belief.

Rushing through a mid-life crisis, like rushing through any complex task, will likely lead to missed opportunities for self-discovery and growth. So, I took the time to confront the big, scary questions and allowed myself to experience all the weird and uncomfortable feelings.

As for coping strategies, I have found mindfulness, self-compassion, and stress management to be crucial. Practicing mindfulness through grounding and breathwork helped calm my mind while treating myself with kindness and understanding during my most challenging moments fostered self-compassion. Humor has always been important to me, but it's also become my favorite tool for stress management, lightening the load and making even the most difficult circumstances seem a little less daunting (like getting in 3-degree water). These strategies were not just theoretical concepts; they became a part of my daily life, serving as a lifeline throughout my mid-life crisis.

Finally, riding the emotional waves of mid-life was a transformative process. I managed to withstand the storms of emotion that come with this phase of life. Confronting these waves head-on, with no shortcuts or detours, has been a grueling yet enlightening journey. It has taught me about my strengths, weaknesses, and most importantly, my capacity to endure. So, I urge you, when you face the emotional waves of mid-life, equip yourself with tools of resilience and embrace them. The storm won't last forever, and when it subsides, you'll find yourself stronger and more resilient than ever before.

Hell, maybe you'll work through yours the same way I have and write a book about it.

Chapter 9: Acceptance

The Beautiful Resolution

I. Introduction (The memoir part)

So here we are, in the final chapters of the book, staring down our mid-life crisis like some freaky deeky duel. If I can give you just a little more advice, don't try to deny what's happening. To get through this one, you're going to have to start accepting that it's happening.

The thing about a mid-life crisis is that it isn't a disease that needs to be cured. It's here, it's inconvenient, and the sooner we come to terms with that, the sooner we can put our big boy (or girl) pants on and deal with it like the responsible middle-aged adult that we are.

Acceptance is such a loaded word and now that we've done the anger, the bargaining, the denial, the 'maybe if I drink enough wine, I'll wake up and be twenty again'. Now, we're onto acceptance.

Acceptance in our mid-life crisis stage is not about giving in; it's about embracing the beautiful catastrophe we've become. Embrace the grey hair - silver is the new blonde, after all. Embrace the laugh lines - because every good joke deserves to leave its mark. Embrace the slower pace - because, let's be honest, our race-winning days are as much a part of the past as dial-up internet.

But, how do we transform this acceptance into a source of strength and peace? For that, we take a deep breath, a leap of faith, and… possibly, a plunge into the freezing abyss of our old friend, the ice bath.

For me, it was only a few months into my cold bath journey that I realized I was already coming out the other side of things. I accepted that I was older, but (again, smaller butt), when I looked in the mirror, I started liking the guy I saw. I think that's where the story changes for a lot of people. It may be your mindset changing, your reflection, or just your brain expanding into this acceptance phase, but I went from looking like, and I quote, "fresh dogshit," to looking pretty alright. It's amazing what a body transformation will do for your psyche.

I don't know what I was expecting when I started putting words down to complete this book, I just knew that I needed to put them down, and now that I have, I couldn't be more grateful. My journey to this point only took a few months, but it allowed me to drop a significant amount of weight, create a daily ritual that gives me a win every single day, and get through my struggle with aging in an amount of time that I can only guess is exemplary.

For your own journey, I can't recommend enough to do something to track your journey. Pictures, video, journal, or anything that you can take a look at in a few months after starting. I've looked back at my videos from the start, listening to who I was, and looking at the transformation of a man lost in his own mind. Today, I have a much clearer view of who I am, where I'm going, and I know I can get there, because I can simply look at where I've come from. If you can face the ice-cold, numbing plunge, you can surely face the fact that yes, you're aging. You may not be as spry as you used to be, but hey, you still got it… no, really!

By now, we know that cold bathing has been the unorthodox therapist I never thought I needed. It's the same with acceptance - it's the unexpected superhero, turning a potential disaster into a source of strength and peace. Who would have thought that we could find the antidote to the mid-life crisis within our shivering, pruned selves in an ice bath? Not me, but life, just like this icy abyss, is full of surprises.

II. The Power of Acceptance

Now that we've dipped our toe into the metaphorical ice bath of acceptance, let's wade deeper, shall we? Just as your heart leaps in shock when that first icy wave hits, so too may your mind reel when first confronting the idea of acceptance.

There's no getting around it, is there? Studies have consistently shown that people who practice acceptance experience lower levels of anxiety and depression, more positive emotions, and a better overall quality of life. We're talking big shots here like Hayes, Strosahl, and Wilson, authors of the book "Acceptance and Commitment Therapy: An Experiential Approach to Behavior Change," who suggested that by practicing acceptance, people learn to defuse from negative thoughts and feelings, to be more present in the moment, and to live in accordance with their deepest values.

Then there's the work of James Maddux, a senior scholar at the Center for the Advancement of Well-being at George Mason University. He found that acceptance of one's mid-life status can significantly contribute to a greater sense of life satisfaction. It makes sense, doesn't it? Acceptance isn't about waving the white flag and giving up. It's about understanding your situation, acknowledging it, and from there finding a path forward.

It's the people who accept their mental experiences without judging them who have better mental health. Less judging, more accepting—kind of like what we do when we embrace the jarring coldness of our beloved ice bath, instead of shrieking in panic and running for the nearest fluffy towel (although that fluffy towel does feel insanely good after).

Think of acceptance as a kind of muscle: the more you practice it, the stronger it gets. And as you flex that muscle, you're better able to cope with life's difficulties. Makes that mid-life crisis look like a minor inconvenience, doesn't it? And just imagine what that can do with the rest of your life.

This is not to say acceptance is an easy path. On the contrary, just like your first few ice baths, and then every ice bath after, it can be quite a shock to the system. But also, like those icy plunges, the more you engage in it, the more accustomed you become, and the more benefits you reap. Acceptance isn't just an abstract idea, it's an active process that can help turn the icy waters of a mid-life crisis into a rejuvenating, albeit bracing, cold tub of personal growth. And that's something worth shivering for.

III. From Resisting to Embracing

If you're anything like me, and since you've stuck with me this far, I'm guessing you are, your initial reaction to a mid-life crisis might be to kick, scream, and generally pitch an adult-sized tantrum. But here's the thing: just like with our frosty friend the ice bath, embracing the shock can be far more rewarding than fighting against it.

Let's circle back to my own "welcome to mid-life" moment. Did I start out zen, calmly greeting the realization that I was halfway through life with a serene smile? Absolutely not! My first reaction was more along the lines of "mid-life, shmid-life, I'm still the spry chicken I was at 20!" But reality has a knack for making its presence felt.

To move from resistance to acceptance, I had to first acknowledge that I was resisting. I had to face the fact that I was in the throes of a mid-life crisis. So, my advice? Stop, look, and listen—to yourself. Recognize that resistance for what it is, and acknowledge it.

Next comes the "acceptance" part of the show. But remember our lessons from the cold: if you relax and breathe, you can get through it. Applying this to acceptance means letting yourself feel your feelings—yes, even the uncomfortable ones. Let them wash over you. It's okay to be upset, to be scared, to be confused. These feelings are all part of the acceptance process.

Finally, remember that acceptance isn't a one-and-done deal. You don't wake up one day, decide to accept your mid-life crisis and BAM, everything's sunshine and roses. It's something you do every day, in small ways. It could be as simple as reframing a negative thought, taking five minutes to breathe, or reminding yourself that it's okay to not have all the answers.

Acceptance doesn't mean everything is perfect. It means you're okay with it not being perfect. And trust me, it won't be. But that's all part of the fun, isn't it? After all, who wants a lukewarm life when you can have a bracing, invigorating ice bath instead?

IV. Acceptance Isn't Passivity

Sorry to break it to you, my sweet angel, but you should know that acceptance isn't a blissful float down a lazy river. It's more like trying to navigate icy, roaring rapids without the cushion of denial to soften the icy plunge.

So, let me be clear: acceptance is not rolling over and playing dead. It's not resigning yourself to the fact that your waistline is more equator than hourglass or that your hairline is receding faster than the polar ice caps. Acceptance isn't about giving up or settling. It's not raising a white flag over your dreams, while dramatically saying "Woe is me!" like some character in a bad soap opera.

Nope, acceptance is far from being passive. It's a bare-knuckle brawl with reality where you emerge bloodied but okay. You look life right in the eye and say, "I see you. I understand you. And I'm going to deal with you, head-on."

Remember my icy cold baths? Well, acceptance isn't about enjoying the chill. It's about diving headfirst into the water, feeling the cold stab at your skin, and understanding that, yes, it's cold, but it's also invigorating, a reminder that you are, in fact, very much alive. You don't stand on the side whining about how cold the water is, you embrace it. And remember, you can do hard things.

So, what does the transformation from resistance to acceptance look like? Start by acknowledging your situation – and be brutally honest. Look at your reflection in the mirror (not the one you've been denying, the real one), and instead of focusing on what you used to be, see who you are now. There's power in that. Tremendous power.

Every day, practice this acceptance. It's not easy – like those icy baths, remember? – but it's worth it. You don't have to like what you see, but you have to acknowledge it. And from there, you can start making changes. You'll realize acceptance isn't a finish line; it's the starting block. And once you're off, the race is all yours. So, take a deep breath, brace yourself for the plunge, and dive into the icy waters of acceptance. It's going to be a hell of a swim.

V. Summary

I learned that accepting my greying hair and less-than-spry moves isn't about waving a white flag, it's about picking up a sequined banner of self-love. I mean, if I can embrace the brain freeze that comes with a daily ice bath, I can certainly accept my love handles, right?

From the academic nerds to the real-life gurus, I dive into the deep end of acceptance, fishing out research that connects acceptance with lower levels of anxiety and a better overall life. Like diving headfirst into an ice bath, acceptance can give you the chills. But just like that numbing cold, it's also strangely invigorating, leaving you with a sense of accomplishment and a renewed understanding of your ability to handle life's curveballs.

Here's the real scoop: transitioning from resisting to embracing is less about turning into a Zen master and more about turning into an ice-dodging ninja. Face it, it's going to sting, you might yell a few choice words, but ultimately, you come out stronger, colder, but invigorated. This isn't about polishing a halo of perfection; it's about accepting the smudged, laugh-line-filled reflection you see in the mirror each day. So brace yourselves, it's gonna be an interesting ride.

In the next chapter of this icy adventure, we'll strap on our snow boots and trudge headfirst into the blinding blizzard of 'Hope.' Don't worry, this isn't about being all sunshine and rainbows about aging – we're past that sort of denial now. This is about spotting the twinkling stars through the storm, the warm cabin waiting at the end of the snow trail, and the cup of piping hot cocoa that makes you feel alive, even with marshmallows stuck to your mustache.

'Hope' is the beacon at the end of the mid-life crisis tunnel, waiting for you to thaw out. We'll explore the exhilarating new possibilities that acceptance opens up for you. Who knew, right? Grey hair and laugh lines aren't just badges of survival, they are tickets to an adventure that makes your heart race faster than you thought possible.

So, dry off, wrap yourself in a warm towel, and brace yourself because we're about to venture into the snowstorm of hope, where the cold never bothered us anyway!

Chapter 10: Hope

The Bright Dawn After the Long Night

I. Introduction (The memoir part)

Welp, here we are at the end, right? Or maybe this is just the beginning?

I think it's the beginning.

When I started this book, on Valentine's Day, I had no idea what to expect on the other side, but as the chapter is titled, it feels a lot like hope.

Nothing about what I've done to this point has been easy, but even sitting down today in my office typing this up, my body feels better than it's felt in over a decade. Strangely, my body feels capable these days, compared to what it did when I started. The pain that I've gone through over the past few months both physically and mentally will forever define who I am, because I'm never going back to that other guy (or how he felt).

In the beginning, there was only pain. My body hurt. My bones, my muscles, my heart, my brain, everything felt like it was creeping closer to the end instead of the rebirth I've created. And yes, this has been nothing short of a rebirth. And yes, it's something I created. Please know that you can create this too. It's not easy, but it's possible if you want it enough.

Looking in the mirror I was disgusted by the overweight and unhealthy man staring back at me. Today, I no longer wake up with sore joints and knots in my stomach. My body listens when I tell it to do something and every part of my life from simply playing with my son, to interacting with my colleagues at work, and the relationship I have with my partner and family has been changed for the better.

While I type this up, I'm looking at my favorite picture of Kirsten and me on my desk, where it will be forever (or framed, I should frame it). In it, she's holding a phone and we're laughing (most likely at me doing something silly on camera). Making her laugh was the best. She had this cozy way of leaning into the laugh where you knew it wasn't just fun for her, it was love AND fun. I really miss that feeling, and her, so much. There's not a single day that she's not hovering right above my thoughts. She's right there and I think the entire family feels it.

Reflecting back at the past 6 months, it still surprises me that I not only went through the physical changes of losing so much weight but that I actually did it in 4 months, with the program I outlined in chapter 7. In February, I didn't change anything, and in March, I was eating a TON… it just happened to be all within one meal. This book will be closed and "marked as done" on August 2nd, six months to the day after I started throwing myself into that cold water.

And for those reading this who know me, you know I've always been someone who does things their own way, but this transformation to me is something bigger and better than any of my previous evolutions. From being on a professional footbag (hacky sack) team to being one of the best numbers jugglers in the world (flashing 10 balls), my activities have never been what-everyone-else-is-doing but they drew me to them. Cold bathing, on the other hand, is the first "fun activity" to me, that has completely reworked my brain.

The biggest change I've noticed is in my mental strength. I now make the decision to do things and then follow through with them without huge conversations with myself about the benefits of each decision. I've seen my patience levels rise when dealing with colleagues, my 2 ½-year-old, and my general interactions with people. And while it could totally be a placebo, I feel sharper than I've felt in years (this could also be because of my general well-being, but it all stems from cold bathing).

This book was never written to pressure anyone into cold bathing or tell you that you need to do it to get to your next stage of life, but for me, nothing has moved me in the way that cold bathing has and I'd recommend it to anyone (who's checked with their doctor first).

So, with all this hope swirling around in my mind and body, I've been thinking about what's next. After doing all of this in such a short time, where do I go from here? Below, you'll find my top 10 list of next goals, a perfect balance of physical and mental tasks to complete.

How fast will I check them all off? No one knows, but I'm guessing by the end of 2024…

Jason's Top 10 List!

- ☐ Hit my goal weight of 175 lbs, by the end of 2023.
- ☐ Finish the next satire (novel) I have in progress.
- ☐ Bike 100 km in one go.
- ☐ Finish the snarky self-help book I have in progress.
- ☐ Complete a half marathon in under 2 hours.
- ☐ Learn. Danish.
- ☐ 100 push-ups without stopping.
- ☐ Cold plunge in a frozen lake.
- ☐ Complete a full marathon.
- ☐ Start writing, Cold Feat volume 2... (when this one sells 10,000 copies)

I think writing it down here will keep me accountable and give *you* a reason to check in and make sure I've done what I said I would in the future. Don't worry, I'm going to check them all off and update my socials along the way.

Also, that last one, if we could bump that up to 100,000, that would be great. Tell your friends. ●

II. Hope as a Beacon

After that warming introduction, let's continue with some psychology 101. Hope isn't just some fluffy, feel-good concept that we toss around to make ourselves feel better. It's a cornerstone of our psychological well-being. It's what allows us to envision a better future, to set goals, and to find ways to achieve them. It's like the lighthouse guiding ships through the storm; without it, we're likely to flounder.

And the transformative power of hope is truly astounding. In fact, according to the field of positive psychology, hope can significantly impact our life satisfaction, resilience, and even our physical health. The psychologist Charles R.

Snyder wrote about this in his "hope theory." It basically says that there are three main pieces of hope, having goal-oriented thoughts, putting strategies together to complete those goals, and being motivated to actually achieve those goals. For me, I just wrote them down, so it seems like my hope theory is en fuego. I hope yours is starting to blossom too.

You might be asking yourself, "Okay, hope sounds great and all, but how does it help with my mid-life crisis?" Well, here's the thing. Remember how we talked about accepting our mid-life crisis? How it wasn't about just accepting our fate, but rather about facing it and our struggles head-on? That's where hope steps in. Hope takes that acceptance and gives it wings. It allows us to say, "Okay, I'm in this thing, but that doesn't mean I'm done. I'm actually just getting warmed up."

Hope is the belief that our future can be better than our present. It's the trust that we have the power to make it so. If you want to read some pretty interesting stuff on this, check out "Breaking the Habit of Being Yourself" by Joe Dispenza. I don't really dig all the discussion of the quantum realm in it, but I can get behind building a future on positive thinking. Hope gives us the courage to dream big, to strive for what truly matters to us, to stand tall and say, "Mid-life crisis? Pfft. I've got this."

I've always had a way of dreaming a little too big for my britches, but for some reason, I feel like it's all a little closer to my grasp than it was before.

So, if you're ready to kick your mid-life crisis to the curb and make the second half of your life the best half, then stick around. This hope ride is just getting started.

III. Finding and Cultivating Hope

That doesn't mean there won't be a good bit of work. Let's roll up our sleeves and dive into the hopeful abyss. Hope isn't a passive bystander in our mid-life crisis show, it's the star of the act. But where do we find it and how do we cultivate it? Allow me to be your humble guide (okay, possibly not "humble" per se, but I've been there, so I can hopefully help).

One surefire way to find hope is to reflect on past experiences where you've overcome challenges. Each of us is a bundle of resilience, full of tales of adversity conquered and trials triumphed over. Reminding ourselves of these instances boosts our confidence and reinstates our faith in our ability to confront future obstacles. For me, every day I emerge from my ice bath, it's a testament to my enduring resilience. If I can withstand 3 degrees every morning, what can't I handle?

No, seriously… I'm a little nervous.

Next up is goal setting, a key ingredient in the hope recipe. Construct a vision of your future - the brighter, the better. What does your post-mid-life-crisis look like? What are you doing, who are you with, where are you? The more vivid your vision, the stronger your hope will be.

For this one, I've recently started writing down what I want (more than just the list above) and really thinking about where I'm going. Paint a map for your life to follow.

Next, hope isn't just about the big picture. It also thrives on small daily doses of positivity. Take time each day to indulge in activities that bring you joy, that spark that childlike excitement within you. It could be reading a book, playing with your dog, trying out a new recipe, or if you're like me, watching your cold bathing friends across social channels get in and/or talk about their own daily dips.

I will not be the first to state this, but cultivating hope is an ongoing process. It requires patience, consistency, and a healthy sprinkling of self-compassion. It's okay to have bad days. Hope isn't about eternal sunshine; it's about believing in the dawn that follows the darkness.

Reflecting on my journey, my sources of hope have been my faith in myself, my determination to face my mid-life crisis head-on, and the little daily victories, like making it out of the ice bath alive and managing to tie my shoes without grunting. They helped me transform my mid-life crisis from an existential nightmare into a catalyst for personal growth.

So, take the leap of faith, dive deep into the pool of hope, and come out brimming with the will to take your mid-life crisis by the horns. Remember, hope is not just a state of mind, but a way of life.

IV. Hope as a Catalyst for Change

Saddle up for the next part of our hope-fuelled journey. It's a mighty force, a powerful catalyst for personal change and growth. Allow me to let you in on how this little beast has played a crucial part in my own life.

Our first stop: the crossroads of hope and change. If change is the destination, then hope is the fuel that powers the engine of our transformation. It's that inner voice whispering, "Hey, things can be better, and you have the strength to make it happen!" This belief in a brighter future nudges us out of our comfort zones and propels us toward positive change.

Now, let me take you back in time, to the pinnacle of my mid-life crisis. Before getting in that cold water, there were a LOT of times that I didn't want to do it. You can watch many of these firsthand on my socials. But then, there was hope, whispering, "Hey, you've weathered tougher storms. It was colder yesterday!" That glimmer of hope pushed me to plunge into the icy depths, ushering in a pivotal change in my journey - the ability to confront discomfort head-on. And let me tell you, nothing prepares you for life's curveballs like a routine of partially freezing your body every single day.

Next up, my odyssey into the world of breathwork. Hope nudged me to explore the quiet corners of my mind amidst the chaos of my crisis. It was a hopeful belief that I could find inner peace, tranquility, and, perhaps, even answers within myself that initiated this change. Today, I can't imagine a day without the ability to breathe properly and the serenity it offers. I'm practicing it right now as I write this and I will in the morning when I row and run. It's a constant, supportive routine.

Our final pit stop, my foray into the realm of fitness. Confronted with expanding waistlines and declining energy levels, hope spurred me on. I think on many of those runs, especially the later runs, hope was known as David Goggins. I haven't mentioned him in the book, but listening to "Can't Hurt Me" really helped me think about not only where I was physically, but where I could go with some real work. It let me change a lot of "I can't" days into, "Yeah-you-cans."

In each of these instances, hope acted as a beacon, guiding me through the fog of my mid-life crisis. It's the little light that sparks the big changes. The whisper that motivates the transformation. It was the steadfast belief in a brighter, happier, healthier future that initiated and sustained these changes.

So, to all you brave souls in the middle of your mid-life crises, let hope be your guide, your catalyst. Let it spark the change you wish to see in your lives. And remember, you're capable of more than you know. If this old man (that's right, I'm embracing it) can do it, you most definitely can! It's time to stop thinking about it and start doing it.

V. Sustaining Hope

Just when you thought we were done with hope, think again! Having a supply of hope is fantastic, but maintaining it through life's roller-coaster ride? That's where the real work lies, and my mid-life comrades, I have some battle-tested tips and tricks to share.

First off, life isn't always a bed of roses. In fact, it can be a prickly cactus at times. Make sure to check in with yourself about what's actually going down. Every setback can most likely be a set-up for a comeback. When you hit a wall, don't throw in the towel. Instead, throw a reality check. Ask yourself, "What can I learn from this? How can I turn this into a stepping stone rather than a stumbling block?" Remember, hope thrives when you believe it can thrive.

Next up? Positive self-talk can boost your hope reserves, especially when the going gets tough. Something as simple as telling yourself, "I can handle this," or "I did this before, I can do this again," can go a long way in fostering hope.

Paint. The. Picture. This is not about wishful thinking but about solidifying your hopeful vision into tangible goals. When faced with obstacles, picture yourself overcoming them. Imagine the triumphant moment when you achieve your goal. The mind can be a powerful ally in sustaining hope if you let it.

Lastly, don't forget to build your 'team.' Hope can be infectious. Spend time with people who inspire you, lift you up, and believe in your abilities. Their hope and positivity can fuel your own. I don't know if I could have done this without all of my cold therapy friends cheering me on, or at least knowing that I wasn't alone in this crazy journey.

Through my mid-life crisis, I've come to realize that hope isn't just a passing thought or a fleeting feeling. It's a lifeline, a steadying force that keeps us afloat when the waves of life get choppy. It's the torchlight that guides us through our darkest hours, showing us the way toward brighter days.

So, my mid-lifer warriors, don't let setbacks dim your light of hope. Keep these tips in your hope toolbox and let them be your guiding star through the winding roads of mid-life. Together, let's embrace hope, bounce back from setbacks, and stride forward into our glorious second act. It's not just about surviving, but thriving through the mid-life crisis! Let's do this!

VI. Summary

In this chapter, I reflect on a personal journey of transformation. Starting the book on Valentine's Day, I embarked on a process of self-discovery and change. My body felt the pain of years of neglect, but I committed myself to a journey of rebirth. Through struggles, I reshaped my physical and mental state, transforming from an overweight and unhealthy man to a strong, capable individual, full of hope. My transformation was influenced greatly by cold bathing, an activity that increased my mental strength and improved my overall well-being. I owe my newfound patience, sharpness, and confidence to this unique practice. Inspired by my journey, I crafted a list of physical and mental goals for the future, ready to continue my path of self-improvement.

Hope was not only the product of my journey but also my guiding force. The transformative power of hope played a critical role in confronting and overcoming my mid-life crisis. Hope allowed me to envision a better future and motivated me to strive for it. It gave me the strength to confront the reality of my situation head-on, reinforcing the belief that my future can be brighter. This, coupled with an ongoing process of cultivating hope, helped me to combat my crisis. Reflecting on past victories and setting vivid goals for the future, I learned to draw upon hope from small daily positivity doses. This way, hope became a state of mind and a way of life for me.

In the next chapter, you'll hear from 13 of the most amazing cold bather's in the world and I'm so thankful to consider each of them my friends.

Chapter 11: The Ice Bathing Club:

The Cold that Warms the Heart

I. The Hall of Fame

The following 13 stories are direct from the horse's mouth. What a weird way to open this chapter… they're actually not horses, they're people. Anyway, the following stories are from the people who inspire me across social media. The cold bathing legends in my eyes.

Each of them brings their experience to the table, some funny, some raw, some intense, but all are amazing. Enjoy them all and then follow them all, I've included links to their deliciously icy social channels before each story.

Stories listed in the order I received them.

1. Shelby Doner, The Cold Water Therapy Nurse
2. Jonathan Lachapelle, Viking Dad
3. Birger Hanzen - birgerhanzen.dk
4. Arjan van der Schoot, Muddy Gnomes
5. Ruud van Holland - Island Iceman
6. Jeremiah Williams - Cold Plunge Colorado
7. Abby Thornton - thornton.spa
8. Jake Ellener - Subzero Jake
9. Brian White - The Plungecast
10. Richard Lee - Unfinished
11. Dylan Oud - Cold Plunge Dylan
12. Tim van der Pliet - TT Breathing
13. James Roycroft-Davis - Recovering Entrepreneur

Just Keep Breathing

Shelby Doner, The Cold Water Therapy Nurse

Connect here:
Website: www.coldplungers.com
YouTube: @shelbydoner

My heart was racing staring at the icicles hanging from the roof. As steam evaporated from my half-naked body, big snowflakes fell softly to the ground. It looked like a winter wonderland. The air was so quiet I could hear myself breathing. I was mesmerized by what I was seeing. The moonlight lit up the clear dark sky. Mother Nature's enchanting yet eerie power and magnificence touched my soul. Suddenly, Drew, my husband, came barreling out of the sauna, "Oh yeah, it's time to get in the cold water! Get in the water, Shelby!" The enchantment and blissful feeling quickly faded.

Ten feet from us was a one-hundred-fifty-gallon stock tank filled with ice and water. A total nightmare to a warm-blooded specimen if you ask me. My husband, for quite some time, had been jumping in it every morning for several minutes and also during our evening sauna sessions. He couldn't stop telling me how amazing he felt and how much it had changed his life! I'd be off to the hospital for work at 5 a.m., and as I'm walking out of the door I'd hear from the cold plunge tank, "Have a good day, dear!" I thought he was completely nuts. Who gets in a tank full of ice water half-naked at 5 a.m.? I'd walk over, kiss him, and say, "You too, please don't give yourself a heart attack."

Every day, Drew would try to convince me to try it. All he talked about was how much energy he had throughout the day and how good his body felt after taking a dip. He even said it was helping lower the stress he had that comes from owning and managing a business. Alarms went off in my mind screaming, "How?!"

I wouldn't budge. I was skeptical and it absolutely made no sense how getting in cold water like that could change your life. Looking back now, I'm being quite honest, I was probably more afraid than anything.

So there I was, on a beautiful December night in 2018 with snowflakes in my hair, staring at my husband meditating in the cold plunge. He breathed slow and deep. The sound of the ice moving in the water sounded like a soft and relaxing melody. You could see Drew's breath as he breathed in and out. Suddenly, the stillness and peace were interrupted when my husband said, "Shelby, just get in the water! Try it!"

I sighed and said, "No, let's go get back in the sauna." He said, "Come on." Keep in mind we had probably had this conversation over a hundred times. I paused and gazed back into his kind eyes. Unexpectedly, I felt a slight urge and motivation inside to cave and try it.

I took a deep breath and slowly put my foot in the water. The cold felt like it was touching my bones. My heart started to beat five times faster as I started to submerge myself. I quickly lost control of my breath and shock took over my entire body. The feeling grew as I swiftly put my arms in so that my entire body was immersed up to my neck. I gasped for air. Fear started to creep in as self-doubt quickly followed behind. Drew kept saying, "You're doing great, just keep breathing." I felt like I was dying and time had stopped. Pain pulsed in my fingers and toes. Seconds felt like hours as my body became energized and shocked by the cold. I couldn't handle it anymore, I had to get out. I burst through the ice chunks and got out of the tank as quickly as possible. I could hear Drew laughing as I ran cradling myself back to the sauna to warm back up. What the heck had just happened?

If I had to guess, I was probably in the cold plunge for less than twenty seconds, even though, at the time, it had felt like an eternity. I sat there on the cedar bench slowly breathing, analyzing my body and the experience. I was completely and utterly dumbfounded. Drew placed his hand on my thigh and said, "Good job dear, now just enjoy it!" My body surprisingly felt amazing and my mind felt light. I could not believe it! I could feel massive amounts of energy flowing through me. I couldn't stop smiling or laughing.

I was hooked.

This moment in my history was a special one. It marked the beginning of something very sacred. Over the last five years, cold water therapy has been such a gift in my life. I have reaped all of the mental and physical health benefits. Not only has it helped me heal deep wounds after losing my father in an accident, but it has connected and brought me closer to so many amazing souls from all around the world.

Depression, anxiety, PTSD, grief, you name it, I have suffered greatly from all of them. I know the darkness and the heaviness they can bring. They can cripple you and make your life chaos. Please know, you are not alone in this journey and you are loved. There is hope for you and you can heal. Who knows, maybe getting into cold water will help you like it did me. It is worth a shot.

Since I began my cold water therapy journey, I have been fortunate enough to help thousands of people along the way reap the same kinds of benefits in their lives. If there is anything my dad taught me, it is to be kind and to help others because someday you might need it too. Love for the world fills my heart and ice baths only magnify that. You can learn a lot about yourself as a person just by jumping into a tank of ice water or taking a cold shower. Ice baths bring out both your weaknesses and strengths. They can be one of your greatest teachers and supporters. The coldness breathes life into your bones if done safely. It is a force that can help you become a better human being. I encourage you to try it, there is nothing like it. If you are scared or have questions, know that I am here for you just like many other fellow cold plungers are. There are cold plungers everywhere, just reach out.

May the cold be with you, my friend.

Finding Light in the Cold

Jonathan Lachapelle, Viking Dad

Connect on Instagram here:
@livewithoutfear.xyz
@ice_viking_family
@ice_viking_dad

It was the winter of 2019 when my world turned dark. A traumatic experience shattered my sense of stability and left me drowning in guilt and despair. That fateful day, I discovered a friend, someone I considered a father figure, lifeless in the snow. It was a sight that would forever haunt my memories.

Only fifteen minutes before, I had spoken to him from the window, promising to put my baby girl, Charlie, to sleep before rushing to his aid. But when I finally stepped outside, it was too late. He was gone, and I blamed myself for not acting faster. The weight of that responsibility bore down on my soul, pushing me into a deep and relentless depression.

For months, I found myself trapped within the confines of my mind. Every waking moment was filled with self-doubt, regret, and an overwhelming sense of guilt. I sought refuge in my headphones, clinging to motivational music and podcasts, desperate for anything that could distract me from my own torment.

However, it was during one of my countless internet searches for a path to healing that I stumbled upon a remarkable man named Wim Hof. Curiosity led me to investigate further, and what I discovered would forever change the course of my life.

In my journey to fix a shattered mind, I promised myself to avoid medication. I had already fought a long and arduous battle with drug addiction, and when I became a father, my determination to stay clean only grew stronger. Medication, despite its potential temporary benefits, carried the stigma of being just another form of substance use that can lead to abuse. I yearned for a natural remedy, something that could help me heal without compromising my hard-won sobriety.

That's when I encountered the practice that would become the cornerstone of my transformation: cold exposure through ice baths. At first, the idea seemed counterintuitive. Why would submerging myself in freezing water have any positive impact on my mental well-being?

But I was desperate. Desperate to break free from the shackles of depression, anxiety, and overwhelming stress. Desperate to regain control of my life and rediscover the person I had lost somewhere along the way. So, with an open mind and a glimmer of hope, I decided to try it.

My journey with cold exposure began tentatively, but as I ventured further into the icy waters, I realized its profound impact on my mind and body. The physical shock of the cold awakened my senses and demanded my full attention, drawing me out of the incessant whirlpool of negative thoughts that consumed me.

Each immersion into the frigid depths became a battle with my fears and limitations. It was a testament to my resilience and a testament to the strength that lay dormant within me. As I embraced the chill, I discovered an inner fortitude that I had never known before.

The practice taught me the importance of consistency. By committing to regular ice baths, I established a routine that provided stability amidst the chaos of my emotions. It became a sanctuary, a sacred space where I could confront my fears head-on and emerge stronger, both mentally and physically.

The cold water became a catalyst for change. It rewired the pathways of my brain, rewrote the narrative of my depression, and forged a new path toward healing. It awakened a dormant vitality within me, a dormant vitality that had been stifled by the weight of guilt and sorrow.

With each session, the cold water eroded the walls of anxiety that had confined me for so long. It taught me to be present in the moment, to focus on the here and now rather than being lost in the remorse of the past or the uncertainties of the future.

The cold became my medicine.

I am incredibly dedicated to bringing awareness to cold therapy because it has played a transformative role in my life, lifting me out of a deep and dark depression. Cold therapy, such as cold plunges and ice baths, has provided me with a powerful tool to regulate my mental health and find a sense of balance and clarity. Through the intense exposure to cold temperatures, I have discovered a renewed sense of vitality and purpose that I am passionate about sharing with others.

Within the cold plunge community, I actively work to educate and empower individuals about the benefits of cold therapy. I understand firsthand the profound impact it can have on mental well-being, and I am committed to ensuring that others have access to this life-changing practice. By sharing my personal experiences, knowledge, and resources, I strive to create a supportive and inclusive community that fosters growth, healing, and resilience.

One of the key projects I am involved in is called "Live Without Fear." Through this initiative, I aim to empower individuals to overcome their fears and limitations, using cold therapy as a catalyst for personal growth. I organize events, workshops, and retreats where participants can experience the transformative power of cold exposure firsthand. By creating a safe and supportive environment, I encourage individuals to step outside their comfort zones and embrace the healing potential of cold therapy.

Social media plays a vital role in my advocacy work. Through various platforms, I share informative content, personal stories, and testimonials, aiming to raise awareness and break down misconceptions surrounding cold therapy. I actively engage with my audience, providing guidance, answering questions, and building a supportive online community. My ultimate goal is to inspire others to explore cold therapy as a holistic approach to mental well-being and personal development.

My dedication to bringing awareness to cold therapy stems from the profound impact it has had on my journey of overcoming depression. Through the cold plunge community, my "Live Without Fear" project, and my efforts on social media, I strive to empower others to embrace cold therapy as a tool for self-discovery, healing, and personal growth. By sharing my experiences, knowledge, and organizing events, I hope to inspire individuals to embrace the transformative power of cold therapy and truly live without fear.

Balance, Health, Strength, and Happiness

Birger Hanzen

Connect here:
www.birgerhanzen.dk

To all my warm friends out there, cold exposure and cold training are incredible for both performance and recovery. It is the natural booster for all you need to live a life in balance, keeping your health, strength, and happiness intact. And then some.

At the same time, the cold represents our laziness, our bad excuses, and a clear indication of how we deal with ourselves. How much we love ourselves.

My journey took 17+ years of consciously and professionally trying to deal with my C-PTSD from childhood. Before this, I trained as an elite fighter and tried to handle my anger in other ways. Then, I found that breathing and the cold could be the most simple and effective 'tools' to heal, hands down.

Both mentally and physically.

After just 3 years of practicing it, I now do it full-time, as a breathwork and cold exposure therapist. Because it does work and it works fast. Days, weeks, or months – not years as I have experienced with traditional therapies.

In 2012, Wim Hof proved that he could control his autonomic nervous system, in 2014 he proved that we all can do what he can do. We can modulate our immune response and deal effectively with acute inflammation.

In Denmark, in 2021 we also proved that this is also the case with chronic inflammation, which is believed to be the root cause behind most of our mental and physical challenges today. And you can do it with just 15-20 minutes of breathwork and 2 minutes of cold exposure, 3-5 times a week.

It's simple, but far from easy. That I know too.

No one ever told us that it would be that "easy." But to this day, it's still hard for me to believe that it's so simple. Just breathe and expose yourself to a few minutes of uncomfortableness.

It's all been proven in so many scientific trials and hundreds of thousands of people have tried it. It should be a no-brainer to start exploring this field.

When I first thought about the practice, I believed that it was only hippies, monks, or yogis who did it, but we all can. And we can do it anytime and anywhere, even when we are busy as fuck, because it does not take that long.

The more you practice it the less time it takes.

In my view, one of the most important pieces of it is that you feel the effect immediately. It's like nothing else I've ever tried.

Find your own method from the principles which are very simple.

Don't trust me - test me. 🤍

The Muddy Gnomes Franchise

Arjan van der Schoot

Connect here:
www.muddygnomes.com
IG: @muddygnomes

Around 10 years ago in 2012, I participated in my first Tough Mudder on Mount Snow in Vermont. This is an obstacle race for adults where you run up and down a mountain and go through a series of military-style obstacles like monkey bars, rope climbs, mud crawls, wall climbs, and going in a big body of water filled with ice. I was captivated by the whole scene and when I got home started to build the obstacles that I had failed so I could practice them so I would do better on the next race and there would be many next races over the coming years. I was hooked.

At the time my kids were attending The Waldorf School in Vermont where in early childhood there is a lot of imaginary play that includes fairies and gnomes. The plan was for me to take some interested parents and teachers on their first Tough Mudder and quickly the team name "Muddy Gnomes" was born. To practice with the team we would come to our house where in our backyard woods I had made a series of obstacles. The Muddy Gnomes came together every week or so to get in shape and have a great time scaling the different obstacles.

Over the next years, we did many races where our objective was always to have fun and not to worry about how fast we were. Nevertheless, I wanted to get better with each year and started to look for body hacks that would help me. One Christmas my wife Charan gave me the book "Breath" by James Nestor in which you learn that breathing through your nose is really the best way to go and that it delivers more oxygen to your muscles and thus you can do more with less. In that book, there was mention of this crazy Dutch man named Wim Hof. Being Dutch myself I was surprised that I had not heard of him before as it seemed that he is quite the celebrity. So next I read "The Wim Hof Method" and in that book it discusses the three Wim Hof principles, the breathing method, cold exposure, and commitment.

So pretty soon I found myself taking cold showers and slowly progressing to having ice baths in our yard. It felt amazing and gave me such a rush. After doing more research on cold exposure and learning about the seemingly infinite benefits that the cold can bring both physical and mental I started to do ice baths more often and quickly other people were joining me. People were excited about doing something as crazy as taking an ice bath but having people come to our house to have an ice bath had some drawbacks and I started to think about a way to take the ice bath experience on the road.

The idea of an ice bath trailer came to mind and after some research online and knowing my limitations I realized I needed help. My friend Mike builds pizza trucks so he seemed like the perfect person to ask. I told him I wanted a trailer that could hold a large amount of water, had a big freezer for ice, room for a few large tubs, and a dressing room. I will get back to you with a number tomorrow, he said and indeed the next day we agreed on a number, and in three weeks he had built the most amazing mobile ice bath trailer complete with eye-catching graphics that included our signature muddy gnomes drawn by another local friend, Adrian.

That first fall I took the trailer out to town and set up the ice bath in the middle of the green. People would walk up to see what this crazy Dutchman was doing sitting in a bath filled with ice and with a smile no less. It was hard to convince people that going into the cold was a good thing but some people were game to try it and almost everyone that tried it became a regular ice bather. A good example of this is my friend Jason who helped out with setting the ice baths up in town. Jason did not under any circumstance want to go in the ice bath but I convinced him to just stand in one for a bit. He took his shoes off, rolled up his pants and after standing on the ice for just a few seconds he said "No Thanks" and got out as fast as he could. He was always game for helping me when I took the ice bath trailer anywhere and after hearing me drone on and on about all the benefits he tried one in the comfort of his own home and was surprised at how amazing he felt. Next, you know Jason set up his own ice bath on his deck and started to take ice baths every single day. Another ice bath fan was born.

At this point, it was all sort of just fun and games since I am not a person who can take an idea to market and do something real with it but that all changed the day I had breakfast with our good friend Staci (Baker) at Denny's. "So, what is going on with Muddy Gnomes?" she asked me. I told her that I should really be starting up a company and get serious about making it a business that spreads the word of all the amazing benefits of cold exposure and taking an ice bath. Staci told me that that is exactly what she specializes in and that she would love to join The Muddy Gnomes.

Soon The Muddy Gnomes Ice Bath Experience was born and we were official. Thanks to Staci we are now going out to different towns and people's homes and to different businesses to provide people with our knowledge of health, wellness, and fitness that highlights cold exposure and the chance to experience an ice bath and feel the thrill of the cold and the camaraderie and team building that comes with that. Everyone that truly takes on the cold and gets in an ice bath while I guide them with encouragement and breathing techniques comes out reborn and most will come back or start their own cold exposure routine.

The response to The Ice Bath Experience is amazing and we are getting to the point where we will be producing more Muddy Gnome Trailers that will be available for franchisees. Soon people all over the US will be able to experience an ice bath and have their lives changed for the better!

Becoming the Island Iceman

Ruud van Holland

Connect on Instagram here:
@ruud_van_holland_
@island_iceman

My coldwater story starts way back in 2001 on the island of Texel, situated in the north of the Netherlands. By the way, my name is Ruud van Holland. On my Instagram account, I show my 103K followers my journey into the cold through my daily plunges in the sea. And it's totally coincidental that my last name is Holland and I actually live in the Netherlands aka Holland.

I wasn't born on the island, but in a small town called Oosterbeek near Arnhem, almost 200 km away from the island. In summer vacations my family and I always visit the island and one day I met this girl who I later married. At the age of 19, I packed up my bags and belongings and moved to Texel. A few years later we bought a house there and since then never moved.

Living on the island is wonderful. It has warm summers and cold winters, in autumn a lot of storms pass the island and every time a storm is coming we go out to the beach to watch the spectacular views of the waves. A lot of tourists visit Texel, mostly Dutch but also a lot of Germans because they're always attached to its pure sea air. And it brings a lot of cash to the island. Texel is well-known for its breed of sheep, Texelaar which was mainly bred for its wool. Nowadays wool isn't bringing in money for the farmers so now they are bred for the meat.

The island is 20 km long and the whole length of the west coast has a light sandy beach where tourists and locals spend their summer days and it's reachable by the TESO ferry.

A lot of locals own a private little beach house and so do we. At the end of September, these houses have to be removed from the beach because of the changes in storms. And so every year in mid-September everything gets packed and taken home to store it for the next season on the beach.

In 2001, I still went every early morning to the beach to take a plunge in the sea. I didn"t had a real plan to do so every morning, it just happened that way. I have to tell you that I suffer from this form of ADHD, which means that my brain is working 24/7, it's a kind of multifunctional computer that doesn't have a switch-off button.

I HAVE MORE THOUGHTS BEFORE BREAKFAST THAN MOST PEOPLE HAVE ALL DAY.

So every morning I'm awake at 06.00 o'clock and I already know what the day brings because everything is already organized and planned days before. Every day has a specific schedule by which I can function. You can imagine it's very difficult for me when things suddenly go wrong or plans aren't going the way I planned them... I get very nervous and I need time to adjust to the new situation.

So like I said, the morning starts at 6, every day. I put on my clothes and drive to the beach. September went by, October came and then November started. In my mind, I was hoping to continue it maybe till the end of this month but I realized my body and mind got used to the slowly getting colder temperatures of the air and sea. Also, the kind of weather didn't make a difference. Sun, rain, wind. Every morning offers a different view and new changes. One of the first things I learned is that it's never too easy to put your clothes down on the sand. I still remember the times I had to run butt-naked after my boxers after the wind blew them away...

Being in the water made me realize how calm my head became. Don't know exactly but the water gave me so much rest I was able to reset my brain and busy thoughts without getting nervous about my daily planning. Combined with breathing techniques I built up my own training, which I still practice today.

In those days I didn't do any research about coldwater training, never read a book about it or searched it on the internet. And yes, I've heard about this crazy Dutch guy Wim Hof who went into the Arctic ice and stood in it for a long time without having injuries or something like that. But I didn't see the benefits of it, years later when I started reading about it everything felt in its place. The benefits I experienced, the boost I got by getting in the cold, the happy feeling after, and the realization I never got sick and Covid 19 passed me by.

Now I read so many books, articles, and papers about the cold and its benefits, I start teaching others about it. In October 2022 I started a group of beginners who wanted to learn about coldwater training and experience the road I've followed since my beginning in 2001. Every morning at 8 we take a plunge in the North Sea, and everybody can join in when they can. So one day there are 4, the next day maybe 12. Some of them have to rush to work after the dip, others have to bring the kids to school, and some of them are retired. Age 21 till 72. I genuinely feel it's so important to tell the members what we are going to do, so nobody is uncertain of what is going to happen physically and mentally. It's easy to tell them about the amazing benefits, but even so important is the knowledge about the dangers of coldwater-training! During the Covid-19 period, many people started taking coldwater dips or ice baths without knowing what dangers there are when people just get in. Shock, brain freeze or breathing problems are the most dangerous situations.

Normally we're quite comfortable having our home at 20-21 degrees. And when it starts getting colder, we turn the heat on. Our houses are well-isolated, with double glass windows, and going outside we wear warm jackets or coats to keep us warm. This is the way we are raised and we're got used to this. And we got more vulnerable to germs and bacteria surrounding us. Wim Hof shows us that when you start embracing the cold it can have a positive influence on our health, and several medical studies at hospitals and universities showed him right. In countries like Norway, Finland, and Iceland it's very common to take cold dips in the winter, and we all heard about the Russian Method when people take short swims in ice cold freezing water. It's part of the lifestyle where the locals learn that we don't have to fear the cold, you can embrace it too. The cold can make you stronger! And that is what I'm trying to teach, my motto for years is :

IT'S ONLY COLD WHEN YOU THINK IT'S COLD!

In all these days doing cold water therapy, doing ice baths, and giving training to others, I realized it's all a part of my mindset. Turn your negative thoughts into positive ones! You can do so much more than you think you can! Stop thinking about not being able to do certain things, start taking the right way to move further! And when you take this new road, so many new options are there to discover!

When you change your way of thinking it's very important you also know what dangers there are. Going into the cold isn't without danger. Hypothermia or drowning. In the North Sea waves are always there. On some days when the wind is strong, the waves are massive and dangerous. One of my rules is to never go in too deep, make sure you can get out before you get in trouble, and never stay in too long! And always choose a safe place where you go in, because that's also your safe way out. And never go alone, take a friend or buddy with you.

I often tell beginners what I felt when I started these cold dips or ice baths in the beginning. Coming out of the water, your body shakes and shivers and you just want to get dressed as soon as possible to warm up again. All the blood from the hands, feet, and other parts of the body went to the vital organs to protect them against the cold so you can survive in these conditions. The shivering means the body takes care of getting colder, the stove has to heat up so the body gets warm again till its normal temperature. And while putting on warm clothes the shivering gets worse and it's so difficult to tie the laces of your shoes. But when you start walking back to your bike or car, you get overwhelmed by these amazing feelings! These are called endorphins and dopamine, the happy-feeling hormones the body starts firing through the body. The first time I felt this was a feeling of thousands of needles starting to prick in my body but in a nice attractive way. I felt so amazing, others call it a boost.

My most spectacular dip is from several years ago, way before the Covid 19 period. Think it was back in 2010 or something. In winter-time when temperatures are getting to a cold freezing period, the Wadden Sea on the right of the island freezes to ice. This side of the island has a calmer sea without big waves so the chances of freezing the water are higher. You have to remember to always check the tide because at low tide the ice is laying on the sand and taking an ice bath then is not really possible. One day years ago I was very excited to take my first ice bath by mother nature. The high tide was in the morning, and getting to the dyke I was so anxious to get in. So I took off my clothes, started walking in my swim shorts and warm hat, got into the frozen ice, and made a hole with an axe.

Thinking about the right way of breathing (fully in, fully out), I lowered myself into the ice and sat there for minutes, enjoying the moment and celebrating my victory. And then I noticed some people staring at me from the dyke and I saw they were nervously talking with each other. The next thing I saw is that some of them started running towards the ice shouting they were going to save me and that I have to be calm! I realized they were thinking I fell through the ice and that this all was an accident... So I quickly stood up and tried to convince them I was alright and this was all planned by me. Never seen so many frustrated people looking at me, standing in ice water in my shorts and hat...

YOU DON'T HAVE TO BE MAD TO DO COLDWATER THERAPY BUT WHEN YOU ARE IT HELPS A LOT!

And so all these years ago I'm driving to the beach every single morning to take a plunge or dip in the North Sea, nowadays with my group. Since I started in 2001 I never missed a day, never got sick, and felt the benefits of the cold water therapy every single time. In 2000 I stopped my bad addiction to smoking and one year later I started my new addiction. My healthy addiction. My cold water therapy. After my daily dips, I come home and take a hot shower, that is my reward. In the end, I always put the water on cold to reset my body and brain. And when I come in after a day's work I often gladly jump into my cold water bath back in my garden.

Our bodies and minds started to sleep during the last centuries. It doesn't know anymore how to function normally because we have taken all kinds of protection against the cold. And that's the main reason people are open to getting bacteria and germs. The bodies are weakened and contagious for all kinds of diseases.

For me, a cold plunge or dip is the perfect start to the day. It gives you the boost or the kick that lasts for the rest of the day. Your body is switched on! So if you want to experience the benefits, the boost, the victory, and that lucky feeling start reading books, surfing on the internet, or look-up in your neighborhood if there's a group of mad people who enjoy the cold water too, find that group of wild swimmers or start your own group of friends and challenge the cold to become your friend too!

Take care and stay safe!

Jeremiah's Believe It or Not

Jeremiah Williams - Cold Plunge Colorado

Connect on Instagram here:
@coldplungecolorado
coldplungecolorado@gmail.com

In 2009 I was watching an episode of Ripley's Believe It or Not and came across Wim Hof, a man they were calling "Mr. Freeze" at the time. Today you know him as the "ice man." In the episode, Wim stayed in a cooler that was -35° for an hour. It was very interesting and left an impression on me but I still wasn't ready to take the plunge yet. It did however plant a seed in my brainmeats that started to grow.

Fast forward a few years to 2017 and I did my first Ice bath in my bathtub. I was trying to get back into athletic shape and I read up on the physical benefits so I decided it was a good idea to at least try. It felt amazing but even then, I wasn't ready to dive in completely, it did get me started taking cold showers on a semi-regular basis though.

Fast forward to 2022, to my first cold plunge at St. Mary's Lake in Estes Park with my oldest Son and my Brother. We stayed in for a little under a minute but I was hooked on that feeling!

I started researching the benefits, not only physically but psychologically. I decided I wanted this to be a part of my daily life so I bought myself a small tub and started plunging daily. I started seeing some pretty profound benefits right away, most notably the absence of depression and anxiety. I also noticed I had more energy than ever before.

An unexpected benefit I found was patience.

l noticed that little things that would have once bothered me or sent me into a tailspin just didn't matter anymore and that felt good.

I did my first cold plunge challenge for February of 2023. I did it to celebrate my sister's birthday on the 28th. I initially intended it to last for 28 days, but I ended up dipping for 80 days in a row!

Cold exposure has changed my life in many ways. Along with fitness, it's helped me wean myself off of my mood stabilizer pills and work through depression and anxiety naturally. It's also helped me be more consistent in other areas in my life and It's taught me that I can do hard things.

The community that I've found in this journey has helped me get through some pretty tough times recently and I'm forever grateful for that.

For you the reader, if you're not sure whether you should get into cold exposure, I say yes! Do your research, but also don't be afraid to just start small!

Why did I start cold water therapy?

Abby Thornton

Connect here:
IG: @thornton.spa
TikTok: @thornton.spa

I'm Abby, 31 years old, and from North West England.

It's a pretty complicated question. I feel like I had a build-up of things going on so where do I start? I became a mother 4 years ago, I'd say from her being one year old I knew she was extra special and she has recently been diagnosed with autism. Before having my daughter I never would have described myself as an anxious person or someone that worried too much but now those feelings consume me.

Not only that, all the women in my family have at some point in their life had a mental breakdown (albeit because of trauma) and I felt like my time was looming.

So I did what any sane person would do. I bought myself a wheelie bin and filled it with cold water. I started cold water therapy in February (bearing in mind that February in the UK is COLD, the water was around 5 to 8 degrees).

I honestly couldn't believe the difference just after a week - my mind was so much clearer!

I'm around 5 months in now and here are just some of the benefits I have noticed:

1. Mentality stronger
2. Not one cold or flu symptom (I've always suffered from colds)
3. Massively reduced my acid problem (I usually suffer from bad indigestion, coughing all the time trying to clear my throat and nausea)
4. Lost weight (not changed my diet)
5. I also don't feel the cold like I used to either

I'm so grateful I decided to log my daily journey to look back on because I can't believe the difference from day 1. The cold community that I've found on TikTok and

Instagram is so inspiring and the positivity that comes from this group is just incredible.

I originally said this would be a 365-day challenge for me but now, I don't think I'll ever stop.

My Everyday Fight or Flight

Jake Ellener

Connect here:
IG: @jake_ellener_96
TikTok: @subzerojake96

My story starts in January 2023 when I first came across a TikTok video of Wim Hof explaining cold water therapy. This sparked an interest in me to learn more about it and to start trying it myself.

I began by gradually adding cold showers into my morning routine. I started with five seconds and carried on pushing myself to stay in the cold shower longer until eventually, I was doing my whole morning shower in cold water. I noticed already that my anxiety levels had started to decrease.

My whole life I had felt out of place and different because I was born with a condition called Cystic Fibrosis (CF). CF is an inherited condition in which, your lungs and digestive system become clogged with thick, sticky mucus. It tends to cause problems with breathing and digestion from a young age. CF over time causes your lungs to become damaged and can eventually cause them to stop working properly. Due to this being a major part of my life, I was always made to feel like I was different from my peers, and this led me down a bad path in life to try and seek acceptance. I was drinking, partying, and doing all the things that were bad for my health to feel like I could fit in.

Eventually, I decided to get away from that crowd of people so that I could start to take care of my health. I took my treatments and this time around I became addicted to running and a healthier lifestyle. At this point in my life, I was taking antidepressants and anxiety medication, on top of my CF medication, which ranged from 15-30 tablets a day. Exercising eventually started to make me feel more confident in myself after I noticed the benefits it was having on my body and mind. Through this newfound love of exercise and positivity, I began to attract people that had an amazing impact on my life.

In March 2020, I met my now fiancée, Courtney, and her beautiful daughter. As we got to know each other more, our relationship went from strength to strength. This made me realize that not only did I need to look after my physical health, but I needed to look after my mental health too. This is what led me to start my journey with cold water therapy.

I invested in a cold pod to fully immerse myself in cold water. I did this every day for two months and after that, I converted a chest freezer into my new and current ice bath. By this point, I felt as though my anxiety was cured. I could feel a boost in my energy levels and my mood.

For me, doing cold water every day triggers my fight-or-flight response, which is the same feeling I felt with anxiety. Deliberately putting myself in a mentally tough situation every day has completely restored my mental strength. It has helped me through day-to-day life, especially when a difficult situation arises.

Cold water therapy has given me the feeling I longed for all those years ago. It has become an important part of my daily routine. I enjoy making videos on TikTok to document my journey and sharing them with a community of like-minded people. Each of them spreads the same message as me: that being uncomfortable is a part of life that needs to be embraced. I finally feel like this is where I fit in, and it's a great feeling.

Welcome To The PlungeCast

Brian White

Connect here:
IG: @theplungecast
YouTube: @theplungecast

December 23rd, 2022. After breaking the ice on the top of the tub with a hammer, I stepped into the 33.4 degrees Fahrenheit water, or 0.8 degrees Celsius for our world readers, and felt the sharp icy truth creeping up my calves to my knees, thighs, and regions I won't mention here for the sake of decency. Did I mention that the ambient air temperature was 6 degrees Fahrenheit, approximately 14 below Celsius? I didn't? Well, it was. I thought to myself, "Brian, this is the coldest water you have ever been in. Let's aim for 3 minutes, but 2 will suffice." As the chunks of ice floated around me, I descended into what would prove to be the most prolific evacuation of breath I had ever experienced. However, because I had worked up to this moment for more than 8 months, my mind knew what to do even as my body tried to re-enact the scene from Looney Tunes, "Roadrunner and Coyote" where the coyote runs headfirst into a painted brick wall. But my brick wall was not painted, and my mind was able to keep my body in place for the full 3 minutes, but I digress.

I can't start a chapter in the middle of a story that might be of some interest. I need to supply the reader with some context, so allow me to do just that. My name is Brian, and at the writing of this wonderful piece of collaborative work, I am 40 years of age. This piece is formative to the story, I promise. My background is piecemeal of medical training in a variety of scopes ranging from operating room orderly back in my undergraduate days, to operating room billing specialist during nursing school, to trauma and cardiac ICU nurse. This last position, which includes a sub-specialty as an ECMO (Extracorporeal Membrane Oxygenation) Nurse Specialist, lead me to my passion and current profession as a Cardiovascular Perfusionist.

If you have no clue what that is, don't worry, you are in the majority. If you want further elaboration, I welcome a pause in reading for a quick Google (stay away from Google images unless you have a strong stomach), but I will provide a brief description here. A Cardiovascular Perfusionist runs the heart and lung bypass machine during open heart surgery and allows the surgeon to work on a completely still, non-beating heart. To keep the patient alive, we place them on this machine that drains blood from the central veins, provides oxygen and removes CO_2, and pumps the blood back into the arterial circulation via the aortic arch. Perfusionists, quite literally, become the heart and lungs of the body while providing adequate anesthesia, drugs, and other medicines, and simultaneously monitoring electrolyte and pH levels of the blood. Ok, I'll stop there. You get it, I'm a mad scientist. It's alive! My favorite part of my job is when we get to take a completely arrested heart, in other words – clinically DEAD – and simply restart it through a series of steps, drugs, and procedures. It's like a beautifully timed ballet of medicine and technology.

My career also involves cooling the patient's body, often to extremes, for humans at least. For complex procedures of the aortic arch, it is not uncommon to cool a patient's core temperature down to a range of 18 – 28 degrees Celsius, or 64 to 82 degrees Fahrenheit. While those are warm paltry numbers in the cold plunge world, I assure you that if your core temperature were to meet those numbers, you wouldn't feel the same way. This is where my expertise meets my curiosity. My cold curiosity began in the late winter months at the beginning of 2022. My wife suggested we watch an episode of a show she already liked called, "The Goop Lab", with Gwyneth Paltrow. This show would typically not be my cup of ice water, I'm not much for tea, but it was the guest who piqued my interest. A man by the name of Wim Hof.

I suspect the vast majority of readers here are well-acquainted with the works of Wim Hof, and the Wim Hof method, so I won't go in-depth about him here. But if you haven't heard of him or are unfamiliar, let me implore you to take time out of your schedule to watch the episode from "The Goop Lab", search his name on YouTube and watch his life story, or just do a quick google of his name and read a little. This man and his method have changed more lives than we may ever be able to quantify. I'll get off my soapbox now.

I watched the episode and immediately knew that I needed to know more. I watched numerous videos on YouTube, read "The Way of the Iceman" and "The Wim Hof Method" within a matter of days, and by the end of the week had signed my wife and me up for a Wim Hof Method introductory course taught by a certified instructor here in Atlanta, Ga. You might say I "plunged" right in. Yeah, I know. The dad joke game is a competitive one and I'm doing my best. After the intro course, I felt empowered to truly begin my breathing, cold, and meditative journey. I had been curious about cold exposure for some time, so I had been taking periods of cold showers to temper my body for a couple of months prior. This is why my wife thought I might enjoy watching the episode with Wim Hof, and she was absolutely right.

I bought a 100-gallon (378 L) Rubbermaid tub and immediately filled it with water from my hose, about 60 degrees Fahrenheit, 15 Celsius. I had purchased a few bags of ice from the store in preparation for the first official home ice bath, and I was excited to plunge into what I expected to be frigid temperatures. The tub was filled with around 70 gallons (265 liters) of water, and I added around 28 pounds (13kg) of ice. My expectations were not met. After about 10 minutes to allow the ice to melt on that early spring day, I checked the water temperature with my thermometer, and it read a mild 55 degrees Fahrenheit (13 degrees Celsius). I still wanted to take the ceremonial plunge, so I did 3 rounds of Wim Hof breathing, found my calm inner quiet, and stepped into the water. This is the part where anyone who has done a first-time plunge knows what is coming.

After the first minute, I was able to slow my breathing to a more life-sustaining rate, and I realized that I was fine, just cold. My goal was 3 minutes, and I met it quite well, finishing with calm respirations and a clear mind. I was hooked. In the months that came after the temperature warmed, I realized that ice was not sustainable for frequent plunging. I purchased a chiller found on a social media marketplace and finally had a set-up that would expose me to real cold temperatures. I stuck to my rule that I created for another 6 months of tempering my body: 3 minutes if in the 30s, 4 minutes if in the 40s, and 5 minutes if in the 50s (I apologize to the worldly readers; 0 to 4, 4 to 9, and 10 to 15 Celsius does not have quite the same ring).

I was experiencing more than simple benefits reported as increases in dopamine, norepinephrine, and the like. I was experiencing a change in outlook, a sense of calmness in my demeanor, and a more deliberate view of life. I also realized that because I was doing this uncomfortable thing over and over, perhaps I could do other things I once viewed as less than appealing. I began running and built an endurance I did not even reach in high school and college. All of this seemed so simple, yet so many live their lives every day without stepping foot into freezing cold water. I needed to find a sense of community, so I started an Instagram page, later carrying my current namesake of "The PlungeCast" to connect with this community and learn and interact with as many people as possible with the same realization that cold can change lives.

Back to December 22nd, 2022. I was excited about this frigid wave of weather as it would provide excellent opportunities for cold plunge content for a guy in Georgia.

This was some of the first content I posted on my cold plunge-focused Instagram page now known as "The PlungeCast." It would be a couple more months until the idea for The PlungeCast would come to me and I would begin producing the content. There was something about this exceptionally cold weather in Georgia that changed my perception of the cold, cold water, and the mind. I began steadily pushing myself to achieve longer times and colder temperatures and listened to my body's response. I was getting all positive biofeedback, so I kept pushing. When I hit my lucky number of 7 minutes in early spring of 2023, I decided that I would fine-tune the temperature a little more to reach the max of my chiller.

So there I was in March of 2023, consistently spending 7 minutes in my cold plunge at 39 degrees Fahrenheit (approximately 3.9 degrees C). It's no record of note and not uncommon, but it felt like the perfect combination of time and temperature had been reached. I used ice to dip the temperature a few more degrees to see if the response changed, but I noticed no difference in my biofeedback. So, what does it mean to find your optimal combination? It means you can become more consistent in your practice, thankful in your life, and feel confident that you are experiencing all the benefits that cold has to offer you. Of note, everyone is different, and each combination of temperature and time will vary. As Wim Hof says, "This is not a contest, and the only competition is within yourself". I am happy to heed the advice of a man who led groups of otherwise untrained individuals to ascend Mt. Kilimanjaro in a fraction of the average time to summit, in minimal clothing or shirtless, after only teaching them his breathing techniques to utilize during the expedition.

I am now in the process of completing my doctorate in Health Professions Education and am developing my research around the educational benefits of cold exposure. I would be humbled to join the ranks of the few Ph.D. researchers who have taken the science of cold exposure as a personal quest to provide new findings to further our understanding of its benefits. I hope to continue The PlungeCast as a project that helps bring awareness and draw attention to the thousands upon millions of people who are waking up to the concept that doing uncomfortable things in life, such as cold exposure, can create new pathways and viewpoints in life and bring richness and context that was not visible beforehand. Flowery language, sure, so in that vein of pontification I will leave you with this thought. If you find something that becomes prolific in your life, such as cold plunging, it is difficult to contain your excitement and desire to share it with everyone. But something I've come to understand is that we must accept that regardless of the evidence, benefits, and literal results we can share, many will look us right in the eye, laugh, and call us crazy while passing by. It's ok. These very well may be the same people who begin their cold journey next year when it finally makes sense to them. "If I can only lend one drop of inspiration to an entire ocean of the embattled, let the ripples reach to the far shores over time as waves of impact."

UNFINISHED

Richard Lee

Follow here:
FB: @Richlee519
IG: @richlee519

A brain injury and how cold plunging helped me… just thinking about writing these notes almost causes me to shut down. For me, it's not normal to expose the personal parts of our lives and be vulnerable. Growing up we are taught that your security lies in your ability to perform, to suck it up when stuff goes wrong, and be stoic, let me tell you the weight of 55 years of that macho bullshit gets heavy.

I am a husband, father, grandfather, son, trusted friend, neighbor, teammate, business owner - those are identities I wear with honor. There is one more to add to the top and that is I am MYSELF… I have recently become aware that I need to retire as a people pleaser.

I was leading a somewhat normal life. Married and raising a family in a quiet rural town south of Ottawa. Establishing my accounting practice, while operating a DJ business for 25 years, we had built our last 2 homes, coached sports, and volunteered in the community. Stress and long days were the way it was. My father passed away from a mysterious brain disease and shook my foundations. I made myself busier, holding fundraisers and establishing a scholarship in his name. I was using many outlets available to me in the form of sports like hockey, mountain biking, and softball until one Friday night in March 2017 when I suffered a serious concussion playing hockey (if you grew up playing hockey, you have had a concussion or three).

Over the next 4 years, I fought ghosts of my old self. I could only work a few hours a day, with dyslexia, speech, and thinking problems, little problem-solving ability, and visual vertigo. I could not sleep more than 3 to 5 hours. No more crowds or public speaking, social events. Dark thoughts set in. TV, alcohol, and snacking became comfortable and I used them as sleeping aids.

Looking for answers and thinking it was partly a motivation thing or something, I hired a life/business coach. When that failed I searched and found references to cold showers, float therapy, meditation, a Wim Hof dude, psychedelics, and various options to explore. Although I would wake up each morning with the hope that I could find a way to get better, I had a feeling that the depression and anxiety were there to stay and that the world could do better without me in it. It's surreal to read those words but that's how easily a depressed and anxious mind makes it seem like a normal and rational thought.

Feb 2021, it was Friday night and we were having a Zoom call, our good friend (let's call her Erin) is raving about ice dipping and invited me for a Saturday morning dip in the St. Lawrence, a river between Ontario and New York.

Saturday, Feb 13th, 7:00 am Cardinal, Ontario, Temp -27 degrees Celsius with wind. Arrived and spectated. Kitsch, Erin, Marijke, and Hendo wade in the icy river, eventually they get out and are laughing and having a great time, I am freezing.

Saturday, Feb 14th, 8:00 am, Manotick, Ontario, Barney McArney Landing, or as the dippers call it, "South Island." The temperature was -15 degrees Celsius. It was a bright morning, we cleared the ice, and one of the dippers (eternal thanks Kitsch) led me in and calmly talked me through the process, that was the morning that my comeback story began.

Positive results were IMMEDIATE and over time I noted several unintended bonuses to cold water exposure. Clarity of mind, sleeping (really sleeping), mood lifted, confidence from doing something you didn't think you could do, quicker healing, boosted immunity (I used to get pneumonia every year, but not anymore).

I rarely go without cold water since that day, right away I attended multiple Wim Hof workshops. I have attended retreats, organized community events to raise mental health awareness, held fundraisers, and really leaned into the wellness culture surrounding the cold water communities in Canada and around the world.

A group meetup on a beach in Perth, Australia showed me the impact a dipping community can have on people's lives. For my 3-month visit, it was like I was at a buffet of self-discovery and development. 'The Human Excellence Project' continues to amaze me with the work they do. Paul, Joe, Solas, and so many others (there are too many to mention and I don't want to embarrass myself by leaving someone out). It was there that I was fortunate enough to spend time and learn much from Nathan Baxter (retired world-class powerlifter, personal coach/teacher, and stroke survivor) and I will be grateful for quality time with Marcel Hof (world leader within the wellness industry, together with his wife Anicha harness a passion to help others, has a brother named Wim.)

Looking forward to this summer to get a dip in the Irish Sea and meet great groups such as RippleEffectIreland (a community that shares the positive effects of dipping), BlueballsIreland (a community focusing on men's mental health), and I'll head to Germany to hop in the Baltic Sea and meet even more local dippers.

I want to be clear that cold water dipping did not fix my brain injury, but it is one of the tools I use to eliminate the symptoms of my brain injury (mental fatigue, depression, anxiety, and lack of clarity) so I have the mental space to continue reworking the wiring of my brain.

Cold water dipping has given me a fair chance at a new life. Most days I have come to terms with the reality that I won't be the way I was, but instead, with enough work, I am excited to see how the new version turns out. Until then, I remain... unfinished.

Becoming Cold Plunge Dylan

Dylan Oud

Follow here:
IG: @ouddy_5000
TikTok: @ColdPlungeDylan

My cold plunging journey started on a freezing cold February afternoon, snow was falling and the air was crisp. It made for a scenic video with so much potential for creativity that I did not realize at the time. I have found a loving and encouraging community through the app that I did not know even existed. Having a community of like-minded people is great for staying connected and sharing ideas. If you don't have a community of some sort whether that is cold plunging, sports, work, or local friends I encourage you to seek out a group that you can be a part of. It has changed my life for the better in many ways I did not know even existed. Get out there in life and carve your own path in whatever interests you. What a journey it has been!

My intentions of cold plunging were more related to the health benefits I was searching for. I will touch more on how the cold water has impacted my health. However, putting it on Tik Tok would keep me accountable and disciplined during my daily cold plunge schedule. By having people who were actively following my journey I felt responsible to fulfill my daily cold plunge routine no matter what. I never expected my Tik Tok page to take off like it has, I now have over a thousand followers and counting. I did not think anyone would watch my content, but I was wrong. People were interested and invested in my journey. I completed 120 days of consecutive cold plunging which has been a great achievement in my eyes. Doing anything 120 days in a row is a great accomplishment. I have since now stopped uploading daily cold plunges to Tik Tok but I still expose myself to cold water daily. I still enjoy posting my cold plunges to Tik Tok but I have shifted my efforts into putting more quality content in my videos which have reduced my daily content to only posting a few times a week. I have enjoyed learning about the video-making process over the last few months. I have improved upon two things during this process: learning how to speak in front of a camera. This is something I have never been good at but participating in my daily cold plunges forced me to go outside of my comfort zone and talk in front of a camera. The second thing I learned was how to edit videos which is something I have found to be very valuable regarding my university studies as I have had to film a few videos for some classes. Going back and watching my videos starting on day one and progressing forward you can see a gradual improvement of the video quality. Not only has cold plunging improved my physical health but I have learned some valuable skills along the way.

The question I get the most is "Why do you cold plunge every day?" which is a valid question to ask. Considering I am jumping into freezing cold water that causes discomfort, I can understand why people ask me this question. My answer has always stayed the same "I do it because it makes my body feel better" which again may sound crazy but it helps me out in many ways. Another question you may be asking is "Why does your body not feel good Dylan?" this question is at the heart of why I cold plunge daily. In January of 2021, I, unfortunately, contracted Covid-19 for the second time which ended up making me quite sick at the time and left me with a variety of lingering symptoms that are categorized as 'Long Covid'. You might be asking what is Long Covid? This is a valid question, essentially Long Covid is a condition where lingering symptoms persist for weeks, months, or even years and is still a mystery to the medical field. I unfortunately suffered and still suffer from various symptoms such as heart palpitations, skipped heartbeats, a pounding heartbeat, shortness of breath, tight chest, tight throat, fainting, fatigue, brain fog, and slurred speech. I suffered from all of these symptoms for over a year. Fortunately, some of the symptoms have faded and now I predominately suffer from a tight throat, shortness of breath, and some fatigue. The closest thing I could compare these symptoms to would be similar to having anxiety or a panic attack but the symptoms never go away. All of these great things in life were suddenly stripped away from me in an instant, I felt frustrated, concerned, and depressed about where my life had led me and it felt like it was all out of my control.

Throughout the past year, I went through three different stages which were confusion, frustration, and desperation. At first, I was unsure of what was wrong with my body, I visited a variety of health professionals and no one seemed to have any answers for me as to why I was not feeling well. At this point I had to take matters into my own hands, I tried a variety of methods to try to feel better. Next, I went through a period of frustration because I was making no forward progress on feeling better. I found it difficult to keep trying when I could not find a way to feel better. Finally, I went through a period of feeling desperate and I was willing to try anything to feel better. This was where I finally stumbled upon cold water therapy and I began my cold plunging journey. The rest is history.

I felt trapped in my own body and no matter what I did I had to live with these symptoms 24/7 which took a toll on my mental and physical health. The most frustrating part is it did not matter what I did I could not regain my prior health. I visited the doctor, the naturopath, the physiotherapist, the chiropractor, the psychiatrist, and my pastor. All of the remedies, tactics, supplements, exercises, and diets made no difference in my health which became more concerning as the months passed. I began to think "Is this my reality now?" I had to drop out of university, I could not work, and I could not play hockey. The symptoms I was experiencing brought me to my lowest point in life, I had zero energy. My heart rate would jump up to 150 beats per minute just by getting up and walking up the stairs and my heart would be pounding out of my chest while I was gasping for air. For the first few months, I lay on my floor all day every day for a couple of months and it wasn't a matter of willpower, I just had no energy to function. However, my symptoms very slowly improved over the next ten months which was progress but extremely slow progress. During this time I researched ways of feeling better, I tried diets, exercise, medication, sound therapy, hot water, cold water, and supplements. Fortunately, I was able to find 4 things that actually made a positive impact on my health. The first was intermittent fasting. I now only eat during an 8-hour window between 12 pm and 8 pm every day. There is something about less food in my body that reduces the severity of my symptoms. I am unsure of why or what the cause is but I know it works for me. Also, fasting is widely known to possess healing properties within the body so there may be some interplay between that and intermittent fasting. Secondly, I was prescribed an SSRI called escitalopram by my doctor to reduce my pounding heartbeat and to calm my body down, which has helped a bit but is not the main contributor to finding relief. Thirdly, I consume a small dose of pure nicotine daily which has a calming effect on my body allowing it to reduce my pounding heartbeat, tight chest, and shortness of breath. Lastly and most importantly is cold plunging, I would say this has been the main contributor to reducing and getting rid of my long covid related symptoms.

I discovered ice baths and cold plunging through a man many of you have probably heard of called Wim Hof. Wim is widely known for being called the 'Iceman" and he may seem crazy to some but to me, he is the reason why I am still here today. I discovered through watching one of his Youtube videos that you can use cold water to activate the Vagus nerve which in turn activates the parasympathetic nervous system which allows the body to rest and relax. After watching that video I thought it is worth a try so I went out and got a chest freezer and began using it to cold plunge daily. Believe it or not, I experienced a significant improvement in my symptoms specifically regarding my heart and lung-related symptoms. I would like to give Wim a lot of credit in terms of me regaining my health, although I am not feeling 100% I do feel I have improved significantly and I can function better in my day-to-day tasks.

I think cold plunging can be used in a variety of ways to help a variety of real-world problems people are facing. I believe cold plunging and ice baths have numerous benefits related to the physical state of the nervous system, heart, and inflammation reduction. However, I think it is also worth mentioning the various benefits it can have on a person's mental state. As for myself, I found exposing myself to cold water boosted my morale and energy levels immediately, it's like you get a hit of adrenaline which makes me feel alive inside. I found I always felt that my mood was boosted after getting in the cold water and doing this early in the morning. it set me up for an excellent start to my day. Which I found to be beneficial because having that good start to my day was good momentum to propel me through any possible obstacles I would encounter throughout the day. Another mental benefit that I received through cold plunging was the combination of discipline and consistency which are closely related. I believe both discipline and consistency can get you anywhere you want to go in life. Motivation can be useful but motivation comes and goes, however discipline and consistency are there every day no matter if you are feeling tired, sick, or depressed you still have to show up every day. I found that by doing cold plunges and posting them on Tik Tok forced me to stay disciplined and consistent because I committed to fulfill. The concept of being disciplined and consistent has also overflowed into other parts of my life such as school, work, and sports which has allowed me to progress and grow as an individual. Cold plunging has been a great addition to my daily routine which I will continue to do for all the physical and mental benefits I receive from it.

I learned a lot through the past year with my health struggles. I think we have all heard the quote "Don't take your health for granted" which has rung true to me ever since I began not to feel well. It is hard to know what you truly have in life until you lose it. I never really understood the significance of my health because I had always been healthy and thought it would continue for many more decades. However, when my health turned for the worse I was sitting in my room thinking I would do anything to be healthy again. At one point I remember feeling so terrible and desperate I told my parents "I would eat a poop sandwich if I was guaranteed to feel normal again" You can quote me on that, it sounds disgusting but that was how bad and desperate I felt at the time. Those were some dark times and some days were extremely tough to get through, at some points I was just trying to get to the next minute of the day that's how bad my body felt. There were some days I thought about suicide because of how my body felt with my heart pounding out of my chest, shortness of breath, and my heart skipping beats, it was pure torture. However, tough times create tough men and I am no quitter, I kept battling through to get to those better times ahead that I was longing for.

On this day, July 15th, 2023, I feel that I have finally gotten to a place where I feel a lot more healthy physically and mentally. I could not have made it through the past year and a half if it was not for all of my family, friends, and God being there for me when I was at my lowest points, I could not have done it without them. I am so grateful to be alive and living this beautiful life I have been given on this earth.

If you have never done a cold plunge or an ice bath I would encourage you to try it, it has changed my life for the better. Start with water that is not painfully cold but cold enough that is uncomfortable. Cold water therapy is not for everyone but it might be something that could benefit you. There is no harm in trying and if it does work for you, you have now found a method that can improve your life that is low-cost and effective. If you are going through a hard time it can be difficult and frustrating which are valid feelings to have. But the most important thing is to never give up and keep fighting however you can. I hope you enjoyed my story and found something to take away from it to better yourself in life.

Tim's Technique (TT Breathwork)

Tim van der Vliet

Follow here:
www.timvandervliet.com
FB: @timvandervliet8
IG: @tim_vandervliet
YouTube: @timvandervliet
TikTok: @timvandervliet
LinkedIn: @timvandervliet

Do you ever have this idea or do you play this game? Waking up in an unknown universe? I play this with my kids a lot. I pretend that I wake up in my own life and look around. I'm like: "Hey, who are you? Are you my child? Am I your Daddy? Oh, do they have a mama too? Wow. She's good-looking." They love it. Anyway, I woke up in my universe once and sat in an ice bath tensing every muscle. Next to me was this bearded guy. A bit of a, no disrespect but, a bit of a weirdo. He was yelling "Right on!" and he was at the same time waving at somebody in the crowd. I tensed every muscle that I could and I stayed in 10 seconds. It was hell. Clearly, my first time in the ice bath I wasn't like, um, how can I say this the best way? It wasn't pleasurable. At all!

I was fighting the cold. With tensing every muscle. You cannot fight something the ice or ice cold water. And this is a bit of a paradox but by being able to surrender to the cold. You get to be stronger and cope with the cold.

Anyway, it took me 3-4 times in an ice bath before I could stay in two minutes. At a certain moment. I had an epiphany moment. An instructor guided me inside the ice bath. The instructor was very close and he looked me in the eyes and said: "slow down your breathing". I was panicking, you know, like hyperventilating. I was able to slow down my breathing. He said: "Now slow it down even more, and more. And more." I slowed it down. And I slowed it down even more and I calmed down completely. And for the first time in my life, I could sit for two minutes in an ice bath.

Now, this is about eight years ago since then a lot has changed. So my first time in an ice bath was with Wim Hof. Then about a year later, Wim and I were in Brighton, UK. We were both giving a talk at the VegFest, a vegan festival, And we were staying in the same hotel and we had a full day together. So we talked for about six hours walking on the beach. The little town of Brighton is beautiful and Wim and I really connected. At the end of the day, we ended up in some gay bar drinking a beer. I said to him: "You know Wim, you're really a brother from another mother, but (tapping my heart) from the same mother planet. Wim said: "Yeah man, still screwed up. But aware this time."

Which I thought was funny. Yeah, man, still fucked up. But aware at this time. I liked that. Although Wim is very famous he's also really just a "no bullshit guy," One time I was on his farm in the east of the Netherlands and he had some kind of pyramid structure to meditate in. I asked, so what is that like? Do you really sense something when you're sitting in that pyramid? He looks at me and says: "no man, it's all bullshit." I like that.

So I became friends with Wim. We have done many coffee, tea, and sometimes beer dates. And then he said to me: "Don't you want to do my instructor course? It will be amazing to have you on my side." And I did the instructor course.

This was intense cold exposure. We walked for 4.5 hours outside at minus 25 degrees. Stayed in an extreme cold cascade for eight minutes. Really intense stuff.

I did it more for myself, for my own development. I had such a fear of the cold. And no, I wasn't planning on being an instructor. But then when I got back from my week in the cold in Poland. I came back, my friend said "ok, let's teach together!" And something started rolling and at a certain moment, I remember I was sitting in my backyard and I was thinking like, "ok, what do I want from life?" The answer was, "I want to travel the world teaching this method." And so I did. I started traveling, to Brazil, the US, Scandinavia, London, Spain, Portugal, and basically anywhere where I'm asked. And anywhere I like to go myself.

Then about six years ago, I became a bit bored of doing the Wim Hof method breathing every morning. So I started designing my own technique based on all that I knew and all that I felt. I thought like, what is the most efficient way of breathing? And that first original version is called TT10. It goes like this: take three slow deep breaths, exploring the depth of your lungs. And then you pump it 10 times in, out, in, out, like really fast and really deep. Then you breathe everything out, you breathe in and you hold and you count to 10 slowly. You can hold longer if you like but a minimum of 10 seconds. It gives a rather trippy effect. Try it! It's like really resetting your brain in a few minutes. It's amazing. Anyway, that was the first time I put out my technique on Youtube.

I started sharing that through Youtube and Instagram and people had the same response that I had. This is really efficient, just feel so much in so little time. It's just amazing. So, I started working on that more. And now after three years, I have my own TT instructor program which consists of in total four levels. 24 weeks of online group coaching and then a week of a retreat. This is at this moment the most complete program to become a breathwork instructor.

I created the program because of 3 reasons:

1. Fast results. TT Breathing is the most efficient way to get out of your head.

2. Many breathwork instructors don't know what they are talking about. WHM instructor teaches WHM breathing only. My program is not only about my techniques. I have guest instructors from other breathwork schools in the program. Essential to be broadly educated.

3. To have an impact on this world. An upgrade for the planet.

Anyway, let's talk a bit more about cold exposure.

So I wasn't the talent in the beginning. Then the most extreme that I did is likely with Wim in Poland. I take two-minute ice baths every time I see an ice bath, I take it easy, keep it simple. Sometimes, especially when I'm traveling, I'm at venues where there's like permanent ice baths and stuff like that. I'm in it every day and within a few days, I build it up to like 8, 10 minutes. Not the first time. My regular training here in Amsterdam is just ending my shower cold whenever I take a shower and I do hot yoga and then a shower cold really long, and really cold afterward as well. I train light yet very consistently.

I've noticed that when I'm like a few months in Amsterdam and I didn't do a lot of ice baths. And then I go to Brazil, for example, there I take like two or three ice baths a day. In the beginning, I have to take it easy, but very quickly, my body is reorganized into more extreme cold training. So within a few days, I can do 8 or 10 minutes. But I never start with it. I train light and never push. This is what I propose, light but consistent training. One of the reasons I went my own way, moved away from the Wim Hof Method, and moved on with Tim's Techniques (TT Breathwork) was that I respect Wim, but I think he's too extreme with his cold training and that it's not healthy. So I take a step back from that and I say light cold training and more consistently brings you long term, much further than pushing it now and giving it up because you train too extreme.

So I guess this was my two cents. Connect with me in any way you like. You can google "Tim van der Vliet" and send me a message.

Why I started cold plunging: My story.

James Roycroft-Davis

Follow here:
www.getwelp.com
www.vulnerablepodcast.podcastpage.io
IG: @james.roycroft

It all started with a glare at the sea. I'd heard of the benefits of cold water immersion several times and never thought that would be me. I hate cold water. Quite passionately in fact! I was always a warm shower man.

But the sea glared at me whilst I was on Christmas holiday with my family on the south coast of England. I was in a rotten headspace at the time. I'd just exited from my last startup after burning out and I was prepared to look for all types of remedies for my mind.

On December 23rd, 2022, we walked as a family with our dogs on the beach and I felt this overriding urge to try cold water immersion. It was impulsive. I'm comfortable with that. So I stripped off to my boxers in front of my entire family. They were shocked, looking at me like I was a madman, but it felt right. I said to my fiancee "I'm going in, time me for 2 minutes" and so she did.

I walked into the sea remembering that you have to keep breathing, my eyes closed, focusing on trying not to die. I got deep enough to cover my entire body up to my head and stood there, eyes closed. I was totally focused on my breathing.

My fiancee shouted "That's 2 minutes James" and I opened my eyes and was shocked at how easy it was to get to 2 minutes by focusing on my breath, so decided I'd stay in for another minute to push myself.

I walked out and my parents were in shock. They looked horrified, concerned, and astonished at what I'd just achieved.

But I was on cloud nine. The feelings rushing through my body were feelings I'd NEVER felt before in my life. Elation. Joy. Amazement. Focus. Cold.

And as I warmed up over the next hour and the highs remained for another five hours, I knew this incredible natural process of cold water immersion was for me. I bought an ice bath there and then and cold plunging became a daily habit.

What I find most extraordinary about this activity is the dichotomy of emotions you experience.

Getting into cold water can be a painful experience. I'd argue there is nobody who enjoys getting into cold water because your brain tells you not to. It tries everything in the book to lead you away from the water in some way shape or form.

I remember the first few times I tried to get into my brand new ice bath were very painful. I told myself I would get up at 6 am and get straight into the water from my bed.

I'd watched Jay Alderton on TikTok and was blown away by the ease at which he rolled out of bed at 6 am and straight into cold water whilst he spoke to camera.

Part of me longed to be like Jay. To have that mental fortitude. To have that strength.

And then I tried doing it. And realized how utterly miserable that type of early process made me feel. Which is strange because I've talked about ice bathing makes me feel the complete opposite.

So I altered my expectations of what the reality is for me. I'm not a 6 am plunger, I'm more like an 8 am plunger when there is sunlight, maybe there's also a slither of hope beaming down from the sky that what I'm about to do won't be painful.

As I get ready by putting on my Budgy Smugglers and my hat, my mind fills with thoughts like: "Should I do this today? It would be so easy not to do this, right?".

But half of this practice, for me anyway, is learning how to allow my mind to conjure up all manner of excuses for something because it's painful, and then to force myself to do the opposite in a controlled way.

That's called brain control and so few people reach that level of mind-body connection, especially in order to control your mind and body to do something initially painful.

I found a practice of mindfulness, part Wim Hoff, part, James Roycroft-Davis improv, which is to shut my eyes and think of the times when I've struggled the most in my life and then think of the times when I've beaten those struggles.

I then take a deep breath in, sit into the tub, and as my body touches the water and I immerse myself in, slowly take a breath out for as long as possible.

This starts the breathing process to control my body's shock reaction to 3c water and from there on in, it's a mind game.

And that's the beauty of the dichotomy; whilst it's a painful experience getting into the water, the feelings after you get in and once you get out are almost like taking cocaine or MDMA. We know the chemical releases in the brain are almost the same as taking drugs. The highs are intense and the longevity of the highs are extensive.

Not to mention the sense of achievement you feel when you come out.

You did it.

That was so unpleasant to start with but you did it.

It's a brain-training cycle of pain and beauty. Tell me where else you could get that?

I'm an entrepreneur with Bipolar and I'm now proud of that fact. Cold water immersion has been a revelation for me because it's given me the opportunity to build a habit out of something I know helps my mental health tenfold whilst also knowing I'm altering physiological processes in my body to help me live longer, prevent disease, and look good for longer.

There is nothing quite like it.

Chapter 12:
Lawyer-Forced Safety Chapter

I. Introduction

My lawyer, who is definitely real, told me if I didn't have a real list of safety tips at some point in the book people could sue me. I was like, "George…" That's a good lawyer name, right? "I don't have money for them to take." And he said they would take the money I don't have yet. Which, I think is ridiculous. But he's the lawyer and below you'll find a letter from him, at a definitely super real law firm.

II. A Word from Our Legal Team

Subject: Importance of Safety Considerations in Ice Bathing

Dear Reader and/or Listener,

I hope this letter finds you in the best of health and spirits. I am writing to you on behalf of the legal team at [redacted], led by our senior partner, George [redacted]. We have been informed about your recent interest in the practice of ice bathing and deemed it essential to reach out to you about the criticality of safety in this pursuit.

Ice bathing, while a potential tool for enhancing health and well-being, is not without its risks, especially if not undertaken with proper precautions. It is pivotal that you understand these risks and adopt necessary safety measures to prevent adverse health effects and potential legal implications.

Firstly, sudden immersion in cold water can lead to extreme shock to the body. This shock can cause heart palpitations, spikes in blood pressure, and rare cases, cardiac arrest. It's strongly advised to have a medical professional assess your health before commencing ice bathing, particularly if you have pre-existing medical conditions such as heart disease, high blood pressure, or respiratory issues.

Secondly, the risk of hypothermia is high during ice bathing, especially without a regulated time limit. Hypothermia can set in rapidly, leading to confusion, loss of consciousness, and in severe cases, death. Hence, it is imperative to have a knowledgeable supervisor on-site to monitor your body's reaction during the practice and ensure you don't overstay your limit in the ice bath.

Moreover, if you are planning to offer ice bathing as a service or a group activity, it is essential to provide all participants with comprehensive information about these potential risks and to have them sign a waiver, releasing you and your organization from liability in case of an incident. Our team can provide further legal guidance and support in drafting such waivers.

We believe in the principle of "safety first" in every activity and recommend you adhere to it too. Embracing this approach, alongside medical and legal advice, will help create a safer environment for you and others participating in the ice bathing sessions.

If you have any questions or need further assistance regarding the legal implications of ice bathing, feel free to contact us.

Stay safe and continue to make informed decisions about your wellness practices.

Best regards,

George [redacted]
Senior Counsel
[redacted] & [redacted] Legal Team

III. Cold Bathing Safety 101

1. Before ever trying ice bathing, make sure that it's safe for you. Check with a healthcare professional: especially if you have any pre-existing medical conditions that could be affected.

2. Gradually acclimate: Start with shorter, less intense cold exposure sessions and work your way up to longer ice baths to help your body adjust.

3. Keep your ice bath duration under 15 minutes: Staying in the ice bath for too long increases the risk of hypothermia and frostbite. I'm a three to five-a-day kinda guy, but it's been stated that you only need 11 minutes a week to reap the benefits.

4. Monitor your body temperature: Be aware of your body's response to the cold and stop the ice bath if you experience intense shivering or numbness.

5. Warm up gradually: After an ice bath, give your body time to warm up slowly. Avoid jumping into a hot shower or sauna immediately, as it can shock your system.

6. Hydrate before and after: Cold exposure can be dehydrating, so drink plenty of water before and after your ice bath.

7. Pay attention to water quality: Make sure the water you're using for your ice bath is clean and free of contaminants (both at home and in nature).

8. Speaking of contaminants: Make sure that anything you use in your DIY ice bath from paint and primer to cleaning chemicals is safe for humans (or at the

very least, organic creatures).

9. Speaking of DIY ice baths: if you're using a chiller or chest freezer, UNPLUG IT COMPLETELY EVERY TIME YOU USE IT. I'm sorry for yelling, but please be smart. Chest freezers were not made to be ice tubs, be careful.

10. Keep a first aid kit nearby: In case of any injuries or emergencies, have a first aid kit accessible during your ice bath session.

11. Supervise children: If children are participating in ice baths or cold bathing, ensure they are adequately supervised and follow all safety precautions.

12. Ask Questions: As you've seen in Chapter 11, there is a huge community of ice bathers out there, if you have questions, ask them before jumping in.

13. Bring a friend: Honestly, every time you ice bath it'd be great to have a friend, but especially in nature, bring someone with you. It gets cold out there and things happen quickly, it would be nice if someone could pull you out if necessary.

IV. What Not to Do in an Ice Bath

Okay, so here are a few things that you should NOT do in an ice bath. I'm not saying I did these things, but I am saying that after doing them, I would probably not do them again. If I did in fact do them. Which I didn't.

1. Don't just jump into the ocean without first getting in and checking if it's deep enough. If you do this, you may immediately hit bottom and hurt your foot.

2. Don't stay under the water so long that it gives you a brain freeze. I mean, do what you want, but the last time I did it, it was the worst. Er… I heard that someone did it. Then again, my hands hurt at the beginning, maybe I need to do it more… hmmm.

3. Do not bring cats in the ice bath. They HATE it. I didn't do this, but it's very clear that most animals would be averse to the therapy.

4. If you're swimming under ice in a lake (don't ask me how or why you're doing this) wear goggles. If you don't, and you open your eyes, you can freeze your eyeballs. I'm not sure if this is true, but I heard it once.

5. Don't eat an extremely hot pepper while cold bathing, there is no feeling in the world like sweating in ice water. Your entire body is on fire, but you're in ice water. You're actually not in any real danger, I don't know, try it.

6. Don't drink and plunge. I actually haven't done this (and am now oddly considering it) but I assume that thin blood AND this wouldn't be very positive. Who knows?

7. If you have one of those really cheap plastic pond basins, don't slide your fingers under the edge as you get in, you'll most likely slide your fingers and it'll hurt while you're in and for days later.

8. Please, please, please, don't force anyone to get in the cold who doesn't want to get in the cold or shame someone who doesn't get in as long as you. I said it before and I'll say it again, this is not a competition. This one is actually really serious and

leads to the next one.

9. Don't be rude, sexist, or racist in an ice bath. This isn't really an ice bath suggestion as much as a life-long idea. Don't be a dick.

10. Don't take life too seriously, no one makes it out alive...

V. Final Thoughts

Hello, you beautiful cold bathing (or potentially cold bathing) son of a gun! I'm so proud of you! Seriously, it's been quite a journey. Even if you haven't jumped in the water yet, the fact that you read or listened to this point is incredible and I'm so thankful for you.

The biggest thing I want you to get out of reading this book is that this is what worked for me. If you decide you'd like to try, please consider not doing it exactly like I did. I threw my ass in ice water out of nowhere and started doing this every single day. I didn't check with my doctor, I didn't ease into it with cold showers, and I didn't do anything "right." As you've seen in my videos, I go hard, and luckily for me, it worked. Who knows if you'll be so lucky?

This isn't a competition, it's a journey and one that you can enjoy for most of the trip. Except for the ice part, getting in the ice water sucks. Every time. Every single time.

Love, Breath, Health, and Ice,

Jason "Cold Feat" Donnelly

Printed in Great Britain
by Amazon